Mommy, Please Don't Leave

CASEY WATSON

THE *SUNDAY TIMES* BESTSELLING AUTHOR

Mommy, Please Don't Leave

Will Seth and baby Tommy ever
see their mom again?

HARPER
element

This book is a work of non-fiction based on the author's experiences.
In order to protect privacy, names, identifying characteristics,
dialogue and details have been changed or reconstructed.

HarperElement
An imprint of HarperCollins*Publishers*
1 London Bridge Street
London SE1 9GF

www.harpercollins.co.uk

HarperCollins*Publishers*
1st Floor, Watermarque Building, Ringsend Road
Dublin 4, Ireland

First published by HarperElement 2021

21 22 23 24 25 LSC 10 9 8 7 6 5 4 3 2 1

A catalogue record of this book is
available from the British Library

PB ISBN 978-0-00-846516-2
EB ISBN 978-0-00-837564-5

Printed and bound in the United States of
America by LSC Communications

I'd like to dedicate this story to all foster carers and social workers, and also to the family support workers and others who dedicate their lives to the service. As far as I'm concerned, these people are some of the forgotten heroes of the terrible pandemic of 2020. Can you imagine having a houseful of troubled children, and then being told you must all be confined to the house 24/7? Teenagers who are used to going out and doing their own thing, toddlers, used to playing with their friends at the park or at nursery, and school-age children who already struggle with learning can no longer go to their place of education. All families have struggled with these problems, but for foster carers it's been so much harder. Some of us barely knew the children who got 'locked down' with us. Some of us had to report our children as missing, even though we knew they just couldn't take being locked down and had gone to meet with a friend. It's been a terrible year for everybody, but I know just how difficult it has been for my particular group of colleagues, and I salute each and every one of you. God bless, and I pray that next year is better for all of us.

Acknowledgements

As always, I need to thank my fabulous agent, Andrew Lownie, and the wonderful team at HarperCollins. Our lovely editor, Kelly Ellis, who has, as ever, been so patient with us and such a joy to work with and also Holly Blood and Georgina Atsiaris. And no thanks would be complete without my eternal gratitude to my friend and mentor, Lynne – who also has the patience of a saint!

Chapter 1

I love a challenge. I always have. And I suspect I'm not alone in that. It's a basic human instinct, after all. Though on this crisp early January day, challenged to find a mermaid for a five-year-old, even I was forced to admit it might be tricky.

Mike and I were on an outing with Annie and Oscar, the twins we'd fostered for a few weeks the previous year. They'd been hard work – how could a pair of lively pre-schoolers ever not be? – but also enormous fun, and uncomplicated too, because they were only in care temporarily while their parents were in hospital, having both suffered serious burns during a house fire. It was our proximity to the major burns unit where they were being treated that had sealed the deal: we were able to take the children in to visit them while they recovered.

We'd kept in touch afterwards. Lovely for us, and also helpful for the family, because it meant Mum and Dad could leave the twins somewhere familiar when they returned to the hospital. Which was something they had to do on multiple occasions, for essential follow-up work. This was one such occasion and, since Mike had managed to wangle a rare midweek day off, we'd taken them to the local Sea Life centre, out on the coast.

Where, apparently, there should definitely be mermaids. Well, according to Annie, who, despite the distractions of dancing jellyfish, bobbing seahorses, anemones, and seals and sharks, was destined to be cruelly disappointed. Not least by her brother, who felt it his duty to keep on remarking that mermaids weren't actually real. 'They're just in *stories*,' he pointed out with the kind of no-nonsense assurance that made it all too obvious who was going to be the one to dash another fervently held belief for her next Christmas.

But next Christmas was obviously still a long way away. And in any case, Mike had other ideas. 'Ah,' he said, 'didn't you hear about the octopus?'

Annie, perched on my hip, better to see into a tank of flatfish, pouted. 'What octopus?'

'The famous octopus,' Mike said. 'The famous octopus who escaped.'

'From here?' Oscar asked.

'From another place just like this. It was all in the news. Everyone thought he'd escaped all by himself – which he might have because octopuses are known for being very, *very* clever – but when they investigated further they found he'd had an accomplice.'

Oscar frowned. 'What's an accomplice?'

'A helper. A special, secret helper. Who'd snuck in in the middle of the night – swam right up one of the big drainpipes that bring in all the sea water – and undone the latch on the top of the octopus's tank, so they could slither back down the drain pipe and escape back to the sea.'

'But how did they know it was a mermaid?' Annie asked. 'It could have just been another octopus, couldn't it? Or a fish.'

Mike shook his head. 'Wouldn't have been able to undo the latch, because fish don't have fingers. Well, that is, unless they *are* fish fingers. And they know it was a mermaid because they found a bit of evidence. A beautiful green scale left behind from her tail.'

Annie's eyes widened. 'Can we see it?'

Mike shook his head. 'Sadly not. They have to keep it in a special box, in a special vault in a museum. If they put it in the light and air – pfff! – it will disappear. And that's why you'll never be able to see an actual mermaid.' He tipped his head towards the play area and the strip of sea beyond it. 'But that doesn't mean they aren't out there, because they *are*. Now then,' he added with a wink. 'Who's for lunch? Don't know about you three but all this mermaid-hunting has made me hungry.'

'You're in your element,' I teased him, once we were installed in the café and the children were colouring in the pictures in their activity books.

'What, water?'

'*No*. Being here, I mean. Out with the little ones. Having fun.' I nodded towards the children, heads close, deep in creative endeavour. 'You know, I miss this.'

Mike looked confused. 'Miss what?'

'Miss doing more of this kind of thing. Miss the children. Miss the grandchildren.'

'*Miss* them? Case, we're not exactly short of children and grandchildren.'

'I know, but do you ever get that sense that it's all gone too fast? That we're spending increasingly more and more time rattling round on our own?'

'Erm, as far as I can see, that day's going to be a bit of a while coming. Carter's not even three months old yet!'

Carter, Kieron and Lauren's second child, and our newest grandson, had been born the previous October. 'Nearer four months,' I felt obliged to point out. 'And yes, I do *know* that. I was just thinking how everything's changing so quickly. Dee Dee in school now. The others growing up so quickly … Can you believe Levi's going to be fourteen this year?'

He slapped a hand down on the table. 'Ah, *now* I get it. You're just feeling sorry for yourself because you aren't in Lanzarote.'

Which was, I had to concede, partly true. Riley and David and our three eldest grandkids had jetted off for a bit of winter sun just after Christmas – a trip I'd have dearly loved to join them on, except I couldn't countenance leaving my own mum and dad when they were both getting so frail, not in the depths of winter, anyway.

And my decision had been the right one, because they'd both gone down with nasty colds over Christmas, which could easily have turned into something worse. But for all that I was busy burnishing my dutiful daughter halo, at the same time, Mike was right – naked jealousy about all that sunshine Riley and co. were enjoying couldn't help, from time to time, but raise its ugly head. I just had to whack it down again, like stuffing a mole back in a hole. We'd promised ourselves we'd get a few days away, late spring. There was just the interminable business of winter to get through first.

Riley was due back in a couple of days, in time for the new school term, and I couldn't wait to have a catch-up, but actually, though Mike was correct about me being envious of the temperatures they'd be currently basking in, it definitely wasn't the whole picture. It was more that I increasingly had ants in my pants; too much time on my hands and not enough family to fill it. And much as I doted on our newest family member, I couldn't monopolise him, because he had other doting grandparents too. One of which – his other gran – was currently looking after him, as she would be doing two days a week now, while Lauren was at work. Which was lovely – they'd moved up here to be closer to them, precisely so she could do so. Which I couldn't resent, and absolutely didn't, but even so …

'Well, yes and no,' I admitted, 'but I think we've been on a break long enough, don't you? I mean, I know we needed it –'

'*And* how,' Mike interrupted, with evident feeling. And not without good reason. Our last placement had been a suicidal teenager, and though it had all worked out okay in the end, the stress of it all had taken quite a toll on us both. My nerves still jangled sometimes, recalling some of the things that had happened. The whole family's did, truth be told. Looking after her had been a particularly distressing and sobering experience, and our need for a long break from fostering had felt very real.

'And I know we said we were in no rush to take on another child just yet,' I conceded, 'but I'm beginning to feel antsy – like I need something to do again. It's probably just empty nest syndrome, I know, but –'

'Empty nest?' Mike spluttered. 'Our house is always bloody full! And – point of order – Tyler's still there. Least he was as of this morning.'

'Yes, and going away for a week in two days, remember.'

'Yes, on a training course with work. It's not like he's off backpacking round the world, love.'

'Yes, I *know* that,' I said, adding in my head, if not my words, that the time might soon come when he'd want to do exactly that. 'But he's an adult now. He's got his own life to live. And with the grandkids getting older –'

'And *us* getting older.' Mike narrowed his eyes. 'Ah! Is *that* what this is about?'

'Yes and no,' I said again. 'I mean, I absolutely don't want to plunge into another full-on placement like the last one – at least, not right now. But –'

'Not *ever* was what I seem to remember you saying at the time,' Mike pointed out.

'I know. But that was then. And I can't just do *nothing*. It's okay for you – you've got your work to keep you busy. And look how much fun we're having today with these two little ones … Admit it, we are, aren't we?'

'A lot more fun that all those sleepless nights worrying about what Harley was getting up to, that's for sure,' he conceded. He leaned over then, and fondly mussed the wayward curls on Oscar's head.

Which I noted. To use to my advantage. 'Exactly,' I said. 'So I was thinking I should call Christine. Let her know I'm up for doing respite again or something. Nothing too stressful. I'll be clear about that.'

'So, do it,' Mike suggested. 'Can't have you moping your way through January. Anyway, you're too young to retire. And I can't see you taking up knitting. Ah, and that's our food order,' he added, as a number was bellowed from the kitchen. 'Clear the decks, kids. Grub's up!' He grabbed the chit and stood up.

And that was my principal thought as I watched him walk away across the café, as tall and fit and strong as ever. That we were too young to retire. That *I* was too young to retire. That I *was* young, full stop. Well, not exactly young. I wasn't in that much denial. But not *old*. Not decrepit yet. Not ready for – that dreaded term – 'slowing down'. And that taking on a little one – maybe a brace of little ones, just like dear little Annie and Oscar

– was *exactly* what I ought to be doing. What I was made for. What I was good at.

Which was probably the reason I reacted as I did when I spoke to Christine Bolton three hours later. Either that, or I'd gone stark staring bonkers.

Chapter 2

Christine Bolton was our supervising social worker. Her job was to oversee the work of all the foster carers on her books, to make sure we were reviewed regularly, kept up to date with any new policies and training courses, and to ensure we were all okay in our day-to-day duties. If we needed anything, or even just wanted someone to rant at, Christine was our port of call. We had worked together for a couple of years now, so she knew us quite well and would always try to match the right children with us. That, at least, was how things were supposed to work. In reality, because of the often urgent need of children placed with the local authority, this kind of matching wasn't always possible. It was more often a case of saying yes first and then learning more about the child as you went along, especially with such a chronic shortage of carers. This then – this scenario of me actually asking *her* for a placement – was a rare one.

'So, you're bored of the leisurely life already, Casey?' she asked, laughing, when I told her. 'I wondered how long it would be. And is Mike itching to get stuck back in too?'

It was early evening, tea done, Annie and Oscar reunited with their parents, and Christine, as ever, was working late at the office. Though her soft Liverpudlian accent held no hint of the pressure I knew she'd undoubtedly be under right now. Christmas and New Year were inevitably busy times, not all Christmases being as magical and glitter-strewn as Christmas cards tended to suggest. And as the last time we'd spoken, we'd agreed to touch base at the end of January, she would, I knew, be glad to hear from me sooner.

'He is,' I assured her, even though that wasn't strictly true. 'Mostly because he knows I'm kicking my heels,' I admitted. 'Riley and David are in the Canaries, Kieron and Lauren are back at work, and now Tyler's working full-time, he's hardly ever here. And I'm bored stiff,' I finished. 'In need of a New Year challenge. And before you ask, I'm definitely not taking up yoga.'

Christine laughed again. 'Oh, Casey, you do crease me up,' she said. 'Oh, and namaste, by the way.'

'Namas-what?'

'Namas*te*. It's a traditional Hindu greeting. And the reason I know it is because I *have* taken up yoga. You should try it. It's done wonders for my back – and more importantly, my mental health. Which has been a godsend, believe me. It's not been the easiest of Christmases this year.'

I'd expected that. The last time we'd chatted had been just before the festivities – in her case overshadowed by her father-in-law's significant deterioration. He had dementia, and she and her husband were facing some tough decisions about his care.

'I'm sorry to hear that,' I said. 'Must be hard on you all.'

She surprised me then by chuckling. 'Don't judge me,' she said, 'but let's just say there's a *lot* to be said for working late at the office right now. No, seriously. We're doing okay. It just is what it is, isn't it? Millions of others in the same boat. Anyway, enough about me,' she hurried on. 'I'm more interested in you. And it's great to hear you're back in the game. I'll obviously put you into the mix. Get word out. See if there's anything –'

'You mean you don't have anything right now?' I asked, surprised. 'I thought you'd be biting my hand off.'

'Oh, I'm sure I will be. This isn't a state of affairs I expect to last, trust me. You know what it's like at this time of year – just the eye of the storm.'

'Oh,' I said, deflated now. 'Well, at least you have a bit of a breathing space.'

'I wish,' she said. 'I'm actually tearing my hair out as we speak. A placement that's proving – hmm – what's the word? Vexatious. That's the one. *Extremely* vexatious.'

'So, can we help?'

'I *wish*,' she said again, more vehemently this time. 'But it isn't one for you and Mike. Trust me, if it was, you'd have been the first couple I would have thought of – even if you *were* on a break.'

Isn't one for you and Mike. Like a red rag to a bull, that. 'Why?' I asked, since I couldn't imagine why any kind of placement wouldn't be. We were supposed to be 'last-chance saloon' specialists, after all. No, not 'supposed to be'. *Were.* 'What's the issue?' I asked her, assuming, in that moment, that the reason she hadn't even thought of us must mean it was something straightforward. Something cultural or geographical. Something practical. Then she floored me. 'It just needs a younger couple, that's all. Which is not to say you're *old*,' she added, as if she'd climbed inside my brain while I wasn't looking. 'But it's a toughie, this one. Demanding.'

'In what way demanding?'

'In every way,' she said. 'At least, that's what I antici-pate. And even with the best will in the world –'

'How? *How* is it going to be demanding? Come on, spill.'

'Genuinely, Casey. I don't think this one's for you.'

'So tell me why,' I said, intrigued, and not a little piqued now. 'Give me all the ins and outs. You've got me going now!'

'I'm not so sure you'll be feeling quite so excited when you hear what it entails,' she said. 'It's one of the most unusual requests I've ever had to put to a carer, to be honest. To several, actually. I'm fast approaching the end of my list.'

'And your tether, I imagine,' I said. 'So go on, try me. At least *tell* me.'

So she did.

And she was right. The long and the short of it was that a nineteen-year-old mother, Jenna, had been sentenced to four months in jail, for drugs-related offences. As a consequence, her four-year-old son, Seth, had gone to live with his maternal grandparents until the release date, and they were apparently struggling to cope. Jenna was expected to serve half of her sentence – eight weeks in total – but with the added complication that she had been heavily pregnant when incarcerated, and had now given birth to another baby boy. 'This one's called Tommy,' Christine explained. 'Born just under a week back. And Jenna still has four weeks of her sentence left to serve.'

So far, I thought, so straightforward. With not long to go, Mother and Baby would presumably spend the remaining time on the prison maternity wing. Not an ideal start in life, but definitely not as bad a start as some I'd encountered. At least Mum and Baby would be clean, fed and cared for. So what was the deal here? To look after the four-year-old till she was released?

My thoughts went immediately to the little ones we'd said goodbye to only hours earlier. 'So I'm guessing you need someone to foster the four-year-old until she gets out?'

'Not exactly,' Christine said. 'I mean, yes, we obviously do need someone to take Seth. But they also need to take the baby. As in the *five-day-old* baby. Which is why –'

'Oh no,' I said, my heart sinking. 'You mean she doesn't want to keep him?'

'No. She does. Desperately so. That's why it's all so complex.'

'How so? Surely she can stay with him in prison?'

'Not in this case. And when she's out, we need her taken on – well, *in* – as well. Which effectively means that, come her release, it'll change from a placement to a mother and baby assessment.'

'Assessment? Are social services planning to permanently remove the children from her then?'

'Again, it's complicated,' Christine said.

And she was right on that, too. There had apparently been lots of activity around the case, the grandparents' inability to care for the four-year-old being the least of it. Yes, that much *was* true, because they both had long-term and apparently debilitating health issues. But the original plan – to obtain a permanent care order for both the four-year-old and newborn, who were both deemed at risk with their 'off the rails' mother – was sent off track by the determination of the young mum herself. Despite a background that flagged her as highly unlikely to be able to care for them she had insisted she wanted the opportunity to prove otherwise, and had a solicitor speak for her, to plead her case to the presiding judge.

'Unusually – no one expected it, of course – something must have chimed with the judge,' Christine continued, 'because she insisted if there was a way to help then we should give her that chance. Hence a mother and baby placement upon her release. As for the newborn, well, you're right, Jenna really could have kept him with her, but she's been withdrawing from some quite powerful antidepressants, and despite her best efforts, according to the medical team at the prison, she's really struggling. Weepy, not sleeping, tired and drained through the day. Not the best combination for looking after a new baby. She also maintains that she wants the best possible start for him, and I think the feeling is that her self-sacrifice in entrusting him to whoever cares for her older son till her release counts in her favour.'

'Wow,' I said, trying to let all the information sink in. 'That poor girl! She must feel like she's got the weight of the world on her shoulders. I'm guessing there isn't a father in the picture?'

'No,' Christine said. 'She's no longer with the older boy's father – surprise, surprise, he's in prison, drugs again – and she's admitted that she's not sure in the case of the baby, and has no interest in, ahem, the candidates, either. But listen, Casey, seriously. This is a *lot* to take on. Just the newborn, on his own, is a *lot* to take on. And a newborn and a four-year-old is a *huge* amount to take on. And from what I've heard the four-year-old is going to be challenging on his own. Then there's Mum, and the fact that the role is going to change. Honestly, this is going to be a twenty-four-seven placement. Which is why I didn't even *think* of you, let alone run it by you in case you fancied coming back sooner. And it's fine. If we need to, we're going to open it out to other agencies. In fact, I was about to do just that when you called.'

'But if I want to? If *we* want to?'

'Casey, seriously now. *Really*? I mean, think. *Really* think. Something like this ... well, it'll take over your life. Is that really what you want? At your time of life?'

She didn't mean anything. I knew that. She was just being sensible. But I did want to think about it. Wanted to be considered for it, seriously. What I didn't want to be considered was too old to cope.

'I don't know,' I admitted. 'But I would at least like to talk it over with Mike. See what he thinks. Can I do that and call you back?'

'I suppose ...' Christine said. 'It's not like you have much competition right now. Just remember what we're talking about. This is a complex situation. If you take them on – take *her* on – you'll have a huge responsibility. You won't just be caring for her and her children – you'll also be the one who determines her future. The one who needs to decide if she gets to keep her boys or not. If you think about one thing, think about that aspect the most. Think hard. Because it will *be* hard. There is no shame in saying no to something like this.'

She was right, there really wasn't. Or wouldn't be, if I did. And a lot of sense in doing so, as well. Because could I? Could *we*, as a family, do this? Mike was currently picking Tyler up from his shift at the local leisure centre, and I knew the first thing they'd urge on their return was extreme caution. But I also knew that, if I wanted to, I could always talk him round. Which made *me* cautious in itself. Because, really, was it fair? This wouldn't be taking on a child. It would be taking on a family. A whole family, and a fragile one, all under our roof. And it wasn't just the responsibility of caring for them, either. It would be the greater responsibility of playing God, or as good as. Of watching over them all constantly, giving guidance and advice, and, ultimately, agreeing to be part of a process that already had no faith in them – that was, no bones about it, probably expecting them to fail and just going through the motions, despite the judge's determination that she be given a chance to prove them wrong. They'd wanted a full permanent care order, after all. And the biggest role of all was the one no carer wanted. I'd have to also trade the role of carer and advocate to that, if it came to it, of both judge and executioner. If my reports made it clear that I didn't think she was up to it, they would use them as evidence that she couldn't keep her kids.

No one knew me as well as I knew myself, and although I often acted first and thought things through afterwards, I was reflective enough to know my own weakness in that regard. Could I do that? If it came to it? Knowing myself as I did? Knowing my blind, often too blind, capacity to love those who others had *not* loved, who thought they were unlovable, who'd been on the wrong side of the track all their lives. It was almost as instinctive as breathing. Could I genuinely be detached enough – at least from the young mother – to do what might be necessary, for the good of the children, to be done?

Forget being young enough, or fit enough. I just needed to be strong enough to make that call. That was the real challenge.

Was I? I awaited Mike's return, deep in thought.

Chapter 3

Mike and Tyler were home only minutes after I'd finished talking to Christine, which gave me little chance to get my own head around what we'd discussed, let alone package it up and tie it in a bow for them both. So, neither happened; I just ran through everything Christine had told me about the case, pretty much verbatim. It was all still so fresh in my mind, after all.

Then I waited, as I habitually did (neither one of them being inclined to speak without thinking, the way I was) and wondered who was going to be first to speak. And to say what I expected them to – that I was crazy, to point out all the likely problems and pitfalls. And, in Mike's case, to wonder how in the space of less than an hour we'd gone from me fancying getting another child in, as I was feeling a bit bored, to suggesting we take on a challenging four-year-old, plus a five-day-old baby, plus their young mother, once she was let out of prison. Irritatingly, though not surprisingly, they both remained silent – as if waiting for me to deliver a punchline.

So, I did. 'So,' I said, 'that's it. And yes, I know it sounds mad. But we have the room for them, we've had plenty of experience with babies and toddlers, and ...'

Tyler glanced at Mike, who I could see was still cogitating. 'She's already made her mind up,' he said. 'I can tell.' He looked at me then. 'You have, haven't you?'

'Of course not,' I told him. 'Not properly. Not completely. Not without you guys being okay with it, of course not. I mean, it *was* you, Mike, who said I should phone Christine and ask about another placement, *and* you did say you were fine with us taking on some little ones.'

Mike tutted. 'Casey, that was not what I said, and you know it. You were talking about doing respite. This is categorically not respite. This could not be further away from "doing respite" if it tried.'

He plopped his keys down on the kitchen counter and went to fill the kettle, pushing his free hand through his hair as he did so. 'Think about it,' he said. 'This all sounds a bit intense, to be honest. I mean, yes, I know we have the room, and yes, we do have enough experience not to be fazed by it, but you can't pretend something like this will be a walk in the park. It's going to mean major changes.' He turned around then. 'This will be hard, love. *Proper* hard. You *sure* you want to take on something this challenging?'

Mommy, Please Don't Leave

Truth was, I wasn't entirely sure and I'd started agonising about it as soon as I'd put the phone down to Christine. It had been almost ten years since our last mother and baby placement, and even back then, when I was ten years younger, Emma, the mother, had run us ragged. Yes, it was true that ten years ago the night feeds, the sound of baby cries, and me being a constant laundry and feeding machine, hadn't bothered me in the slightest, but the nurturing, the monitoring, and the reporting back of everything Emma had or hadn't done had made me feel awful. I'd felt constantly torn, split down the middle between heart and head, because no matter how much I had wanted Emma to succeed, my duty was to record and report any and all of her failings. It was the hardest thing I had ever had to do, and the first time I'd ever felt part of a system that was just waiting for someone to do exactly that.

Well, not exactly. Deep down I knew that of *course* that wasn't true. Everything was set up to give a mother every chance; all they had to do was follow the rules and the examples set. But how many mothers – even the best mothers – could hope to be that perfect? Every new mother fails at some things at some point, which is why a second child always feels that bit easier. And for mothers like Emma, so young, and so lacking in support and family role models, how could the scales not help tip towards failure? And being scrutinised to such a level while experiencing one of the biggest learning curves a human *could* experience … well, it was no wonder the odds were against them. It was that more than anything that had made me want to try. If I could keep those little ones out of care, wouldn't it be worth it?

And she'd succeeded. That was the main thing. She'd had so much stacked against her, yet she'd proved the doubters wrong. We were still in touch. She had turned her life around. She had come through.

She had set a precedent. That was the main thing. Not least where I was concerned. With my thought processes, right now.

'I think I do,' I said.

Tyler grinned. 'See, I told you, Dad,' he added.

'No, but listen,' I said, as Mike began assembling mugs. 'These placements only last for around twelve weeks, as far as I remember, just like an assessment period while the local authority decide what to do. So even if it is hard – and I'm not under any illusions about that, trust me – it will only be for a limited time. And if it's plain the girl won't be able to cope they'll end it by default at the interim court hearing in any case. And if it all gets too much for *us* – at any stage in the process – then we call Christine and say *we* need to end it. We do have that option. It's not like an open-ended placement, is it?'

Mike rolled his eyes. 'Like you'd ever do that,' he said.

'I know. But if we have to, then I will,' I said. 'I promise.'

Which was, or at least looked like, the end of the conversation. I had been all braced for fielding a raft of objections or, at least, considerations, before we plunged straight on in. And nothing.

'So?' I said.

'So if Ty's happy, I'm happy,' Mike said. 'Ty, you happy?'

'Happy,' Tyler agreed, with a nod. And – *was* it that? – a slight smirk?

I looked from one to another. '*What*?'

Mike glanced at Tyler, then rolled his eyes, and smiled. 'Just a little wager, that's all.' He passed me a mug of coffee. 'Love, if you're sure you want to do it, then we'll do it. I think it'll be tough, maybe even tougher than it sounds, but even given *that*, I suspect it'll be preferable to you turning Christine down, not now you know all about it, about those little ones. I think that's something we can agree on, eh?'

'You're probably right,' I began. 'Still, I –'

But something had evidently just occurred to Tyler. Some important detail that he'd previously not considered.

'Mum, the mother, yeah? She's not going to be, you know, *breast*feeding it, is she? You know, like Lauren does with Carter – you know, as in in the lounge and the kitchen and all that? Because that would be *weird*.'

I almost burst out laughing at his mortified expression. 'No, love, she won't be. At least, I'm ninety-nine point nine per cent certain she won't, anyway. The baby would be coming here a month before her, wouldn't he? Pretty tricky to breastfeed remotely.'

He was blushing to his roots. Eighteen going on fourteen, I thought, but didn't say. Easy to forget how late a starter our boy was. But equally easy, given his start in life, to understand why as well.

'Phew,' he said. 'That's alright then. Okay, I'm cool.'

As was Mike, and, in that short time since I'd told Christine I would think about it, so was I. Too cool? Perhaps. But I was one for following my instincts and they were telling me the same as Mike was; that if I didn't take this little family in, now I knew about them, I'd probably regret it more.

So it was that while Mike caught up with the late news, and Tyler headed off upstairs to pack for his training course (he was being picked up by his boss at seven the next morning), I phoned Christine back to tell her that we were up for it. Though not before establishing what the 'wager' had been about. Ty's analysis of the scenario that would likely greet them when they returned. That I'd have made up my mind to do it, as in agree to a new placement, that Mike would suggest we didn't act in haste, that I'd promise that I hadn't, and wouldn't, and would happily turn it down if he said no to it. And then we'd do it anyway. 'Because that's what *always* happens, Dad,' he'd apparently pointed out.

Ouch.

The following afternoon, which Mike had hastily arranged with his boss to take off as annual leave, we were stationed by the living-room window, both clutching cups of coffee, waiting for the imminent arrival of little Seth. He was being picked up from his grandparents at lunchtime and was being brought to us early afternoon, to give him time to settle in (well, at least, to adjust to his new reality) before his baby brother was brought to us a couple of hours later. Because that in itself was going to be a major change for him. Though he had been old enough to understand that his mum was expecting another baby when she was taken away to prison, the reality – that he was no longer her only child, and that he now had a baby brother – was a big change for any child, let alone one who'd already seen a lot of upheavals in his young life, and been parted from his mum for a month now already.

Mike was pacing, as was his habit, wearing out the same old strip of carpet. Calm as he was, he was always a bit tense at such moments, perhaps because they represented the point of no return. We'd be getting what we were getting and there was nothing we could do about it – or at least so much less than we could have before this point, possession not only being nine-tenths of the law, but also the point, in the sense of us taking possession, where to extricate ourselves would all be so much more difficult.

Happily, a car pulled up while there was still a little pile left on the carpet. 'That's them, now,' Mike said. 'That definitely looks like a social worker's car.'

We had never discussed by what rationale he decided what a social worker's car looked like, but he was invariably right so I put down my coffee and took my habitual deep breath as I watched a slim young man unfold himself from the driver's side and, having retrieved a passenger from the rear of the car and a holdall from the boot, re-emerge onto the pavement, closely followed by a sweet-looking little boy. 'So get away from the window then, you loon,' I said. 'Let's not have them thinking we're as mad as we actually are. Come on.'

The child was already marching up the path as we opened the front door to them. He looked slight, pale of face and had severely cut hair, and wore a matching hoodie and joggers in a lurid shade of green. 'Well, hello!' I said, by way of greeting, while the social worker caught up. 'I'm Casey, and this is Mike, and I imagine you must be Seth?'

My big smile remained glued, even though he completely ignored me, pushed resolutely past both of us and marched onwards into the house.

'Baby Tommy! Baby Tommy!' he yelled, first towards the stairs and then again as he marched on into the living room. He was a skinny little thing, but he had a bulkier boy's swagger. 'Where are you, Baby?' His voice was sing-song. 'It's your big brother, Seth!'

I focussed on the social worker as Mike followed the boy through the house.

'Does he think the baby is already here, then?' I asked.

'Sam Burdett,' the man said, putting down the holdall, and smiling as he held out a hand to shake. 'And yes, I assume he must do, despite my telling him at least six times that the baby's arriving later.' He lowered his voice slightly. 'He sort of works to his own agenda, this one. Clearly didn't believe me.'

The big smile remained in place, as such smiles must in such circumstances. As the social worker now edged past us, too – albeit with a 'sorry' – in pursuit of his diminutive but confident passenger, who had now re-crossed the hall and gone into the kitchen. He looked young – mid-twenties absolute tops, I judged – to be in the job he was doing. But perhaps he just had a very youthful face.

We both followed along, to find the social worker in the act of getting down on one knee. 'Listen, Seth,' he said, kneeling beside the child with a friendly hand on his shoulder, 'remember I told you Baby Tommy was coming a bit later? It's just you for now, remember? So that you can get to check out this new place before your brother gets here. How cool is that?'

'Piss off!' the child shouted, immediately ducking away from Sam's hand and swiftly kicking him in the shin for good measure. It would have been slightly comic, were it not for the fact that the child's eyes had filled with tears. Angry tears, frustrated tears. Tears that looked pent-up, and born out of genuine distress. 'This is a shit holiday,' he sobbed. 'I wanna go back to Grannie's! And where's my fucking brother? She said my brother would be here!'

I rushed forward to try to salvage the situation and also to try and calm Seth, who looked as if he were about to have a major meltdown. 'Hey, Seth,' I said, as gently as I could above the din. 'I'm Casey, as I said. And this here is Mike. And we've both been *so* excited about meeting you. And I tell you what. I have orange juice and blackcurrant squash, and a whole tin of different biscuits to choose from. How about I get you a drink and biscuit? Would you like that?'

He considered me warily, his eyes still angry, his arms stiff by his sides. 'Are they chocolate?' he demanded. 'I only like chocolate biscuits.'

While Sam Burdett returned to a standing position, seemingly happy to let us take the initiative, Mike shot to the cupboard and produced the tin of chocolate biscuits – posh ones, too, left over from Christmas. 'They are indeed,' he said, brandishing it, 'definitely the ones you like. But come on,' he added, in response to the little hand reaching out to grab it, 'let's sit down for a second and eat them at the table, while Sam tells us all about you, how about that?'

My mind was going ten to the dozen, trying to take everything in that I could about our tiny new house-guest. *And* his keeper. The child had obviously been told he was coming on holiday, which was usually a big no-no in my book, but all too often used with younger children, in order not to worry them too much before they were delivered. Had it been the right call here? I wasn't sure. He was angry, defiant and clearly not afraid of saying whatever he wanted to anyone, and using whatever language he chose to. So, was this evidence of the challenging behaviour I'd been told about, I wondered? Or just a reaction to the immense upheaval he was experiencing?

Whatever the truth of it, Sam Burdett seemed stressed, and I began to visualise the hour's car journey he must have had getting Seth to us. And then the reality that he seemed to know almost nothing – either about the child, or the case he'd been given. 'I just have this,' he explained, pulling a two-sheet care plan from the inside pocket of his jacket, while Seth tried to stuff an entire chocolate biscuit into his mouth in one go. The term 'biting off more than you can chew' came immediately to mind. 'There'll be more, though,' he assured us, as Seth wandered back off across the hall. 'When they bring the baby, later on, they'll be bringing much more information,' not adding, though it was written so plainly on his face, that as he was the newbie, he'd been given the rubbish job. 'As you can see,' he did add, nodding towards the living room, 'Seth isn't taking this very well at all. To be honest, despite the conditions at his grandparents, he was adamant that he wanted to remain there.'

'Conditions?' Mike asked.

Sam Burdett's immediate response was to grimace and shake his head. And his next – because he clearly didn't want to say anything inappropriate – was to simply add 'not good', and sigh knowingly.

'As I say,' he finished, 'my colleague has much fuller information, and will brief you properly later. But, in the meantime, if you need to get in touch, my mobile number's on the care plan.' And then, give or take a nicety, he was gone again, only adding a brief 'Be good' to Seth as he passed him.

Mike and I looked at each other in silence and turned back to Seth just in time to watch him deliberately push over the side table in the living room, complete with the two mugs of still-cooling coffee, sending it spilling all over my beige carpet.

'That was an accident,' he explained, smiling for the first time since he'd arrived. 'Don't hit me. Or I'll call the cops and have you shot dead.'

Chapter 4

The next hour felt like four as Mike and I played an unintentional game of 'follow Seth'. A game we would come to play daily in the following weeks, and one which we learned would inevitably cause us no end of stress.

'Where the hell has he gone now?' Mike called from the hall. 'He can't have opened the front door by himself, can he?'

The door had both a key and a Yale lock, which meant a two-handed operation. So that, at least, shouldn't be a worry. Well, in theory. I scanned the living room. Seth had been right there with us just a minute ago and I'd only turned my back to scrub the stain off the carpet while Mike took the mugs back to the kitchen. I joined him in the hall and turned the key to check I'd double-locked it anyway. Then took it out, and put it on the high shelf above the coat rack. 'Just in case,' I whispered, 'and, Mike –' I lowered my voice even further. 'The kid is only four, but he will most likely be listening and enjoying the fuss, so let's not make one.'

Instead I decided to try out something I recalled doing with my Riley and Kieron when they were little. The dramatic 'I really don't care' technique. I winked at Mike so he'd play along.

'Oh, wow,' I said *sotto voce*, 'at last! All nice and quiet. Shall we go have a sit down and watch *PJ Masks*?'

To be clear, I had absolutely no idea what *PJ Masks* was. But I had at least scanned the two A4 sheets that had so far comprised our new guest's 'paperwork'. And there it had been, near the top of the 'all about me' section, listed as his favourite TV programme.

Not knowing this, Mike gave me his usual 'what the hell?' expression, but was happy to play along, because he could see I had a plan, not least because I was mouthing 'I have a plan' at him.

'*PJ Masks*!' he said. 'Woo hoo! My favourite!' He then followed me into the living room and grabbed the remote control.

Readers, I should proudly announce at this point that we now had what I call a really posh television. It's wonderful. All you need do is speak into the remote control and say what you want to watch, and it finds it for you! Mike still thinks it's funny that I use my telephone voice to operate this amazing device, but I like to be polite, even to machinery.

'*PJ Masks*!' I said, as Mike held down the speak button (I no longer added the word 'please' to my requests as I now knew this was why I could never find the right shows), and just like magic, a whole row of episodes appeared for us to choose from. Mike selected one at random and pressed play, then we turned up the volume and sat back to watch the colourful little superhero characters on screen. Sure enough, within minutes, Seth had crept quietly back into the room and was now kneeling on the rug, seemingly oblivious to us, his head resting on his arm, on the coffee table.

Five minutes in, I decided to try to engage him. 'Oh, I love Owlette,' I said, having identified what looked like a key character. 'I wish I was her. Who do you like best, Seth?'

'Catboy, but sometimes Gekko,' he said, without turning his gaze from the screen. 'But you can't be Owlette. My mummy's Owlette.'

This felt good. Like the first smidgen of progress. 'That's okay,' I said, 'I just like her, that's all. But, Seth, do you want to sit up here on the sofa to watch? I have a really soft blanket you could curl up under.'

Seth turned to look at the fluffy blanket I had pulled from the side of the sofa, and then seemed to be gauging the seating space left next to me and Mike.

His head swivelled, then returned to me. 'Can you two go in there?' he asked, pointing towards the kitchen. 'And I have the sofa for just me?'

I knew Mike must have been itching to get up and leave anyway so I smiled and nodded. 'Course we can,' I said, as we rose from it as one. 'And then later, you can tell us all about what we missed, can't you? Though we'll leave the doors open so we can still hear it, okay?'

Seth, half his attention back on the screen again, nodded and scrambled up onto the sofa, pulling the blanket around himself like a cloak. 'And can you bring me a drink in as well?' he asked, again, not really looking at us. 'But I need a baby cup with a lid, cos I'm fucking gormless.'

'Jesus Christ, Case!' Mike said, as soon as we were in the kitchen and out of earshot. 'What the hell kind of household has he grown up in? I thought he was with his grandparents. How can that kind of language be part of his everyday vocabulary?'

I nodded, feeling very grim about it all. I'd once before had a child with a similarly colourful vocabulary – an angry, almost out-of-control five-year-old called Paulie, who'd been cruelly rejected by his mother and stepfather. It had been an eventful few days – but at least it *was* only a few days, and it dawned on me now that this particular potty-mouthed pre-schooler was going to be with us for a fair bit longer. And during that time, as a consequence, I wouldn't be able to have our own grand-children round. I simply couldn't. They couldn't see this as normal behaviour, and the little ones were too young to realise it wasn't. So if they heard it they would almost certainly pick it up, just as Seth had. I could have kicked myself for not having thought about this before. This placement had now, at a stroke, become just that little bit harder than we had thought.

'Well,' I said, slightly disinclined to share my thought process with Mike yet, 'we can only hope that being away from that environment, and being in one that is so completely different, might change all that. He might forget all those words.' I shrugged. 'At least, that's the theory. But I really don't know if we should make a point out of telling him off when he swears, or just ignore it completely and give him other words to use by repeating what he says without the cursing.'

Mike shook his head. 'I think we have to actively stop him, love. If he speaks like this in the home, then he'll do it anywhere, and we can't have him thinking that's normal, we just can't.'

'Another thing,' I said, 'speaking of normalising things. I think I made a mistake in putting the living-room telly on. We really ought to get them their own telly. Their own space. The family, I mean, when Mum joins us.'

'Leave it with me,' he promised, but with the air of a man who had decided we'd made a mistake, period.

Shoot me down in flames but there are always going to be times when the TV is a justifiable, and also excellent, childminder. This was one such time, because Mike and I then enjoyed almost three-quarters of an hour of peace as Seth avidly watched episode after episode of his favourite series, seemingly locked into his own little world. Luckily I had found a plastic 'baby cup' in the back of one of my kitchen cupboards; almost unbelievably, it had belonged to my oldest grandson, Levi – who'd be fourteen this year, I reminded myself for the umpteenth time. Yikes. It still had his name on it, albeit very faded, but it did the trick and made me feel righteous, for once, about hoarding so many of the baby things 'just in case'.

It seemed like no time at all then, before we heard another car pulling up outside. 'That must be the baby,' I said, smiling at Mike. 'Oh, I can't wait to see him.'

He grimaced. 'Well, at least he won't have learned any four-letter words yet.'

Leaving Seth where he was, we both went to the front door to greet them, and I was surprised to see what looked like the same car that had arrived earlier. And more so to see Sam Burdett step out of the driver's side, before opening the back door and retrieving a small, presumably occupied, baby seat. A young woman then appeared from the passenger door, went round to the boot, and pulled out a suitcase and two large supermarket shopping bags. Babies, I reflected, never travelled lightly.

They came up the front path, looking for all the world like young, slightly frazzled parents – well, at least Sam did. He definitely looked sheepish as he introduced the young woman. 'This is Lizzie Croft,' he said. 'Lizzie's a family support worker. Sorry for the confusion,' he added sheepishly, presumably referring to his own reappearance, 'but I wasn't aware that I'd be back when I was here earlier, or I'd have said so.' Though what he had to be sorry for, I didn't know. Then he clarified. 'I mean I'm social worker to *both* children, not just Seth. I just assumed that because Lizzie was collecting Tommy from the prison, that I wouldn't be needed – I thought she'd be bringing him straight here.'

I smiled at him in a way that I hoped conveyed that he had no need to be nervous. 'Well, the more the merrier,' I chirruped. 'Come on in. Let's all go through to the kitchen. Seth's watching TV right now. Thankfully.'

Lizzie Croft smiled as she passed me, clearly as pie-eyed about newborns as I was. 'Isn't he *adorable*?' she said. 'We've been playing pass the parcel with him at the office. Such a poppet.'

'A lot more adorable than his older brother,' Mike whispered, once he'd ushered the little party into the kitchen.

I liked Lizzie straight away. Just on instinct and first impressions. She looked to be in her mid-thirties, and seemed genuinely warm and friendly; the sort of woman you just knew really, really enjoyed her job. I also liked how she was dressed – jeans and cowboy boots, T-shirt, leather jacket. To me that said a lot about her attitude to the work she did. No-nonsense attire for a no-nonsense, no airs and graces job. Down to earth and approachable – definitely my type of woman.

She proved me right, too, as she efficiently took the baby from his car seat, quickly stripped off his blue quilted all-in-one suit, held him up so she could smile at him, and then passed him to me. I didn't yet know if she had her own children, but I suspected so.

'And this,' she said, in the voice we all tend to use when talking to babies, 'is little Tommy. Oh yes it *is*! Isn't he beautiful!'

At which point, Seth appeared, just as I was nestling the baby into the crook of my arm.

'Is that my baby?' he asked, marching in a beeline straight towards me. 'Where's my mum then?'

Lizzie lowered to a squat and twisted around on the balls of her feet. 'Remember me, Seth?' she said brightly. 'We met yesterday at your grannie's? I told you how Baby Tommy would be joining you here today, didn't I? But Mummy won't be here for a while yet.'

Seth stared hard at Lizzie, and then at Sam, before coming right up to me and inspecting Tommy closely. I held on tight, braced for any trouble – there was no telling how he'd react – as he held Tommy's little hand and raised it a little.

'What does he do then?' he asked. 'He looks like he's dead.'

'He's asleep,' I explained. 'He's only very tiny so he doesn't really do anything much yet, except sleep and drink baby milk and have his nappy changed.'

Seth was unimpressed, clearly. 'What's the point of a brother who just plays dead?' he asked. 'You can send him back. I want one who talks.'

Poor Lizzie, who was squatting still, made the mistake of laughing. And paid for it, too: Seth immediately swung his fist and hit her straight on the nose. And as she struggled not to topple sideways, he kicked her in the knee for good measure.

'What you laughing at, you fucking slag?' he yelled. 'You're a lying slag! Where's my fucking mummy?'

I watched, helpless and horrified – and still holding the baby – as Sam pulled Seth away and Mike helped Lizzie to her feet. Sam had Seth in his arms at chest height, with the boy's back towards him, and I cringed as I watched Seth repeatedly kick backward, his heels making repeated contact with his young social worker's groin.

Sam could hold him no longer then – he was clearly in too much pain – and as he let him down, he doubled over in agony. And Seth, apparently oblivious to the pain he had caused, took the opportunity to run out and go thundering up the stairs, screaming abuse – 'Get me out of here! I want my mummy! You're all slags!' – the whole way.

'Well, that's us told,' Lizzie said, gingerly touching her nose. Then grinned wryly. 'The joys of social work, eh?'

'Speak for yourself,' Sam just about managed to splutter.

Yes, I thought, but didn't say, as we ushered the pair out. *As in, you two get to leave. And we don't.*

Still, there was nothing to be done because that was what we'd signed up to. Or, rather, *I* had, and dragged everyone else along, in my usual optimistic fashion. 'Here,' I said to Mike, keen to seize the initiative, 'you take the baby. I'm off upstairs to set some boundaries.'

He held his hands up, rather than out, and shook his head firmly. 'If it's all the same to you, *I'll* go up and set the boundaries. While *you* ...' He wrinkled his nose and started fanning the fetid air in front of me.

Then, leaving me with the baby, and a distinctly noisome nappy, he hurried off up the stairs.

Chapter 5

When Mike returned after going up to check on Seth, he didn't look happy.

'Is he asleep?' he asked, nodding towards the baby in my arms. 'Because if he is, you're going to want to put him in his baby seat or give him to me while you go up there and see what Seth's been up to. You just won't believe what he's done to his room already.'

I felt a familiar gloom descend. We weren't more than a few hours into this yet and the scales hadn't so much fallen from my eyes as drilled down into the centre of the earth. How long had the social workers been gone now? I wondered, as I trudged up the stairs. Ten minutes? Perhaps even less than that. And in that short time Seth had clearly waged war on the bedroom. All the toys I had carefully set out for him were strewn everywhere, including a full box of Duplo. A fairy story book that had once belonged to my granddaughter Marley was now missing half its pages – they'd been turned into confetti

– and, as I scanned the room, I could see Seth was poised for further mischief – he was just about to draw on the wall with a purple colouring crayon.

I stepped forward and pulled it from his grasp just in time. 'I'll take that,' I said. '*Thank you*. What on earth are you doing, Seth? Why are you spoiling all your things?'

'They're *not* my things,' he barked back, little fists clenched by his sides. 'I don't care! They're not *my* things! I *hate* them!'

I'd been yelled at by more angry children than I could remember, so it was water off a duck's back on an emotional level, but on a practical one, if I was going to be in a position to help *this* shouting child, I needed to think on my feet. Was this simply an urge to destroy anything he could lay hands on, or had the toys themselves inflamed his anger further? Yes, he was frustrated and disorientated, and perhaps not in the right place to be cheered up with playthings, but some children, particularly if very young and with a background of extreme neglect, could become genuinely overwhelmed and distressed around toys – many because they were psychologically overcome by such an astonishing degree of choice and plenty, and a tragic few because they simply had no idea how to play. But this child? I knew conditions hadn't been ideal at his grandparents, but did he fit that mould? I didn't imagine so. But imagining would get me nowhere. I would have to strip it all back a bit before I would find out where and who he was. And before I could do so, I first needed to concentrate on consistently establishing those boundaries.

'That's fine, Seth,' I said, adjusting my voice to a firmer, less conciliatory tone. 'If you don't like any of these things, then I'll take them all out of the room. I'll just leave your bed and cupboards if you think that would be better. But in the meantime, we do *not* throw things all over the floor. Do you understand?'

Seth eyed me for a moment, before preparing his body for battle again, fists clenching tighter, tiny milk teeth barring, face pinched. But this time I refused to engage with it.

'Of course you understand,' I continued. 'You're a big boy who is four, not a baby.' I bent down and picked up the book, before looking directly at him. 'Come on! We need to pick all this stuff up. It's almost teatime and I need you to help me, okay?'

I didn't know if it was my tone or the mention of food (he really was a skinny little thing, to the point of looking under-nourished), but the anger left his face immediately and his shoulders relaxed, as if furiously destroying things and helping with tea were just two of several options on a list of activities, and seamlessly switching between them was as natural as breathing. Then he obliged me with a smile – real or fake, I couldn't tell yet – and said, 'I can help with tea, Mrs –' he frowned. 'What's your name again? My grannie said I'm good at sandwiches. Shall I make us jam sandwiches?'

I nodded. 'Yes, you can. Absolutely.' I took a punt then. Held my hand out. Seth grabbed it immediately and, seemingly, happily.

'Come on then, kiddo,' I said. 'And you know what? We'll tidy up after tea instead. And it's Casey. Do you think you can remember that? *Cay-see.*'

Seth nodded. 'And what's the daddy called?'

'Mike,' I said, smiling. 'Come on, let's see if the daddy wants some jam sandwiches, shall we?'

We got through the rest of that first day somehow, including a Mary Poppins-style tea of jam and bread, followed by biscuits and blackcurrant squash (needs must – we could bring in other food groups tomorrow, I reasoned), during which Seth's eyes began markedly drooping. So, dispensing with earlier plans to give him a nice sleep-inducing bath, we instead opted to take full advantage of the situation and popped him straight into bed in his joggers, taking off only the hoodie, leaving him with just the grubby T-shirt he had on underneath. (Duly noted, in terms of his grand-parental care.)

Then, having completed only a speedy – and noiseless – tidy-up, we went back downstairs to raid the fridge for something a little more sophisticated to eat, and enjoy some uninterrupted cuddles with Tommy, who was so far proving to be the complete poppet he'd been billed as.

Though a poppet who didn't come with the usual given – that at the end of the day Mum or Dad would be taking him home again. Which had me immediately in a state of mild stress again. How much formula did newborns drink? How many night feeds did they need? I'd had all my grandkids for sleepovers from a pretty early age. But not *this* early. The last newborn we'd been in sole charge of overnight had been Kieron and, as I remembered it, it had consisted of short bouts of slumber, regularly punctuated by trips to his little nursery (in response to some imagined noise or other), which often involved putting a hand *very* carefully on his back to check his lungs were still moving up and down.

Mike laughed when I shared my anxieties with him. 'What the hell happened to your famous "instincts"?' he said, guffawing. 'Seriously, love, stop fretting. Just *follow* them, and you'll be fine.'

And, of course, he was right. It definitely helped that we'd decided to have him in the bedroom with us until his mother arrived – not least because his brother was an unknown quantity, obviously – but maybe because a woman's body simply remembers and adjusts. Mine certainly seemed to. I woke every couple of hours or so, alert to the slightest sound, which gave me time to slip downstairs and microwave one of the previously prepared bottles, then get back to the bedroom and pick him up for a feed before he'd even cried out. And all while Mike slept like a baby himself. Nothing changes.

I also found it ridiculously easy to fall back to sleep myself, so after the 4 a.m. bottle I drifted off almost immediately, buoyed by a conviction that this bit wouldn't be so hard. Yes, it would be tiring, but it wouldn't be for long and, as Mike was increasingly fond of saying these days, we could sleep when we were dead.

Or, in Mike's case, sleep *like* the dead. It felt like only five minutes later when I was suddenly jolted awake by him sitting bolt upright in bed and going, 'Whassup?'

'Whassup' was Seth, who was apparently banging on our bedroom door. 'Lady! *Lady! Man!* I need *breakfast!*'

Both Mike's hair and eyes were wild. He was clearly confused. He'd obviously forgotten that we now had two little house guests. 'What the hell is going on?' he asked blearily.

Then the penny dropped. Not least because a sudden anguished cry came from what had formally been a space on my side of the bed. Mike sighed heavily and rubbed the sleep from his eyes. 'Remind me again,' he mused, 'why we thought this would be a good idea?'

He didn't seem to require an answer, so I squeezed his arm instead, then, since the baby was already awake, I reached to ping my bedside light on, but then thought better of it. My bedside clock read just after 5 a.m., less than an hour since I put the baby back down. Perhaps I could get him back to sleep again. It would at least allow me to give Seth my undivided attention for a bit while Mike got ready for work – something I knew might be key to a slightly easier life.

'God, I *hate* these dark mornings,' I whispered, as I swung my legs round to the side of the bed and plucked the mewling baby from his cot, marvelling, just as I did every time, at just how minuscule and fragile-feeling he was. 'Would you mind taking Seth downstairs, love?' I asked Mike as the banging outside the door continued. 'Your alarm will be going off soon anyway. Maybe give him a drink to be going on with and put the TV on for him, and I'll follow you down once I've settled little one again?'

'Harrumph,' Mike huffed and puffed as he hauled himself up. 'That's one *very* imaginative definition of "soon".'

Once Mike had gone to work, and I was down to just the one pair of hands, I stumbled through the morning much like any frazzled new parent is apt to do. A new parent managing a newborn and a very angry toddler. Seth might be four but 'angry toddler' was his default mode currently, and there was no getting around it – he had every justification. He had been uprooted from his normality and dumped with a stranger, plus a baby brother who, bottom line, meant next to nothing to him and, in the absence of his mother, must have felt a very poor replacement.

So I felt for him, hugely. Which went a long way towards mitigation of his wearying behaviour, which consisted mostly of asking incessant, angry, sweary, and mostly hard-to-answer questions; at least in a way that would be appropriate for him, such as '*Why* did my mummy leave me?' and '*Why* can't you take me back to grannie and gramp's?' In fact, the only time he wasn't angry was when he wanted something from me, and would switch, instantaneously, to 'full-on cute' mode.

Polite, no bad language, and disarmingly charming. This was learned behaviour, clearly, and I was surprised that a child so young could have learned to be manipulative in such a way, but it was also a glimpse of the sweet little boy he might have been all the time had life not dealt him such a rotten hand of cards. It was a blessing that little Tommy was at that very early life stage where his needs were simple and easily met; perhaps he'd escape such psychological damage.

Needless to say, the five hours that passed between Mike leaving the house and Christine Bolton arriving at it felt like an eternity. Just five *hours*, and I was already mentally drained. Thank goodness the baby, currently sleeping in his baby seat on the kitchen counter (I took him and the seat everywhere with me, including the loo, to be on the safe side), seemed to be content to mostly sleep away the periods between feeds. If he was fractious too, it would make everything so much harder. Though there was obviously still time for that.

'You're a sight for sore eyes,' I told Christine as I opened the door.

She laughed. And then remembered herself (and the situation) and winced sympathetically. 'That bad?' she asked as she followed me from the kitchen – to get Tommy – and on into the dining room, and sat down.

'Who are you?' Seth asked, eyeing Christine suspiciously. 'You look like the social.'

I'd dressed him in his choice of the other outfits he'd arrived with. A little grey hoodie, with matching cuffed trackies and one of several pairs of *PJ Masks* socks. He had put the hood up immediately and kept it that way all morning, strutting around with that pronounced swagger I'd noticed when he arrived with us, looking as if he really *was* from the 'hood. I wondered if his grandfather had given him the buzz cut.

Christine laughed again. 'Well, I *am* a social worker,' she said. 'My name's Christine, and you must be Seth.'

I should have seen it coming but I didn't. Seth made a throat-clearing sound and then spat on the carpet. 'Fucking social,' he snapped at her. 'Sticking their noses in our business. Fuck off, slag, we don't need you round here!'

'That's enough, Seth,' I said sharply. 'You do not spit in this house, and I won't have you talking like that either.'

I swept him up then, almost instinctively, using my usual 'time out' principle, and immediately saw the fear in his face. His body stiffened against me, presumably braced for a verbal reprimand. Or worse? Another instinct took over when I thought that, which made me reconsider; this little boy was lost, rightly anxious about the appearance of another stranger, and obviously just parroting something he'd heard. And it was all trotted out so easily I knew it must be something he'd heard often, and was simply mimicking, so I mentally flagged it up for consideration later and, from Christine's expression, guessed she was doing the same thing.

With all that in mind, I relaxed my grip, and hoisted him onto my hip koala-style instead. 'Come on, don't get upset. Let's put some more *PJ Masks* for you while me and Christine have a cup of coffee, okay?'

My reaction seemed to surprise him so much that not only did I get a grin but even a peck on the cheek, as I settled him on the sofa and selected his programme. I knew I was being manipulated – this was presumably his way of thanking me for not telling him off when we both knew I should have – but these little moments were all helpful, both in terms of information and communication; adding detail to the picture of the behaviours I was dealing with.

Leaving Christine minding Tommy (a luxury in itself), I then went into the kitchen to make us hot drinks and when I returned, she had one of his tiny fists wrapped around one of her little fingers, despite the fact that he hadn't apparently stirred. 'Incredible how they do that, isn't it?' she mused. 'How the instinct is so strong. He didn't even wake up.' She grinned. 'More's the pity. Actually, no. What am I saying? You have your work cut out, don't you? Is there anything you need?'

'Besides a straitjacket?' I joked, 'I'm not sure. But I am aware that Seth is old enough for nursery – shouldn't he be going to one?'

Christine nodded. 'He really should but it's complicated. His old nursery, by all accounts, were glad to see him leave. He was barely there most of the time, but when he was there, he was a nightmare – and all the other kids were apparently scared of him. But you're absolutely right, and it's his right to be in education.' She nodded a second time. 'And we need to sort it out. Different local authority complicates it, but we should be able to circumvent that, and we will. Can you hold out for a week while we get it organised?'

Knowing I had no choice in the matter, I could do nothing but nod as well. 'Do you have any more background paperwork?' I asked, hopefully.

'Not as in actual paperwork,' Christine confessed, 'since they're so new to the system, but I can at least fill you in on what I do know.'

Which didn't make for very encouraging listening. Conditions at the grandparents had apparently been 'dire, to say the least'. She painted a picture of a household I could so easily visualise. Filthy carpets and surfaces, liberally strewn with empty beer cans and glasses, cigarette-filled ashtrays, a kitchen sink well on its way to being a site of special scientific interest, empty fridge, empty cupboards, and nothing whatsoever for Seth to play with, bar a selection of the above.

'And there wasn't an inch of clear floor space, either inside or out, where the poor kid could play anyway,' Christine added. 'There wasn't even a bed for him, just a stinking duvet laid on the floor of a tiny bedroom, and another one on top to keep him warm. It was *awful*.'

And this from someone who had seen many kinds of awful in her career. 'But of course *they* had their home comforts. Internet, smart TV with every channel. Endless supply of booze and fags. I don't know how they got away with it for so long. Mad thing is, they were the ones who phoned *us* and complained that they couldn't handle Seth. I mean, really? As if it never even occurred to them what we might think when we got there? And I genuinely don't think they could care less. Not about the state they were living in. *Or* their grandson.'

I noted the edge in her voice, and could guess what she was thinking. She'd lost her own daughter to cot death, so to see evidence of such indifference to a helpless child must have affected her personally. 'Anyway,' she hurried on, 'turns out they only decided to call us in when they found out that they couldn't claim benefits for him without it getting complicated. Questions being asked and so on. That's when they decided he had to go.'

I looked across at the little boy sitting not three metres away from us. 'Sounds as though they never wanted him in the first place.'

'I suspect you're right.'

'God, no wonder he's like he is,' I said. 'Poor little mite. Still, maybe when his mum comes here he might be better?'

Christine frowned. 'Much as I hate having to hear myself say it, I wouldn't count on it, Casey. Apparently – well, at least according to the grandparents, anyway – he hates his mum, kicks and screams at her, and calls her all kinds of nasty names. They blame it on her choice of boyfriends; said he's picked up all his colourful language from them. I think the general impression is that they don't have a lot of time for their daughter. They're older parents, too. Markedly so. Perhaps they couldn't handle her. It certainly seems odd that, not long after she had Seth, she moved out of the family home. I mean, she was still so *young*. It speaks volumes, doesn't it? Still, at least she has her flat, so if she does prove everyone wrong, she can at least return to her own place.'

It did speak volumes. Not least in regard to the troubled little boy we were taking care of, who I now noticed was getting up from the sofa. 'You okay in there?' I called out. 'Has your programme finished?'

'I want a drink,' he said, stomping to my side, eyeing Christine as he did so. 'In my big boy cup.'

Interesting. Last night he had called it a baby cup. But he definitely meant the same one because he trotted across to the draining board and pointed to it. He looked pointedly at me then, and I understood immediately. He didn't want Christine to think he was a baby. He wanted her to think he was big.

I filed that thought away to ponder later as well. It might help me to strategise, getting this kind of insight into what made him tick. 'Oh, your *big boy* cup,' I said, going over to pluck it from the drainer. 'Of course. You want purple or orange in it?'

'Purple.'

I filled the cup, made sure the lid was on tightly, and handed it to him. And once again, he caught me entirely unprepared. Because no sooner had I given it to him than he lunged towards Christine and lobbed it at her head. The lid stayed on thankfully, but still, being full, it hit her with some force.

'I told you to fuck off outta here,' Seth yelled at her, 'I hate the social. They took me from Grannie and now she's sad!'

I felt terrible for Christine, whose head I knew must have really hurt. I'd more than once been accidentally clocked around the head by an over-excited toddler with a sippy cup, so I knew how it felt. She rubbed her forehead vigorously, but remained impressively composed, and I knew she was purposely minimising her reaction so his behaviour wasn't rewarded by the one he'd sought, despite her clear need to give him a reprimand. 'That wasn't a very nice thing to do, was it, Seth?' she said calmly. 'I'm sorry you feel sad.'

'Grannie's sad, you idiot, not me!' Seth raged, 'I'm mad! I'm gonna get the cops and get you done!'

Once again, I picked the livid little boy up and deposited him back on the sofa, then pointed my finger at him to indicate I was serious. 'Now you sit there and calm down,' I warned. 'That was a very naughty thing to do and we are going to need to talk about it afterwards. In the meantime, you sit there until you can say sorry to Christine.' I walked back into the dining room, where my supervisor was still rubbing her head.

'I'm so sorry, Chris,' I said. 'Are you okay?'

She flapped a hand at me. 'Oh, I'll be right as rain,' she said. 'It's *you* I feel bad for. I mean I knew there were behavioural issues, but I wasn't told anything about him being so aggressive. You wouldn't think he had it in him, would you? Little dot that he is.'

She would now. Though I opted not to regale her about yesterday's antics with her colleagues. It would only make her feel worse, after all. And I had *dealt* with worse, often, from much bigger, stronger children. 'Well, if the family were under the radar, which it seems they were, then how could you know? And who's to say he exhibited this kind of aggression with his grandparents anyway? It could all be a reaction to events. Just, please, try your best to get a nursery place round here for him. That will help so much.' I smiled ruefully. 'More than you know.'

'Oh, I'm learning,' she said. 'Anyway, I'd better make tracks.' She started gathering up her bits. There was a little lump forming on her forehead.

'That looks painful,' I said.

'Oh, it'll be fine,' she reassured me. 'Though I think I'll pass on the farewell with Seth. And I'll catch up with you later and, please, if you need anything, even if it's just someone to rant at, just give me a call, okay? Day or night. I *mean* it. Anyway,' she finished, nodding towards the still-sleeping Tommy, 'any chance of waking this little fella up? I can't possibly leave here without having a cuddle.'

I unclipped the clasps and took Tommy from his baby seat for her. He really was the most beautiful, loveable little thing. So perfect. But with such a horribly uncertain future. I handed him over. 'Here you go,' I said. 'Fill your boots. I think you've earned it.'

Chapter 6

As every parent and carer knows, one of the key things with babies is that they need to be settled into 'a routine'. And since 'routine' should have been my middle name (with 'clean-freak' my first name) this was obviously always going to be my mission, so I spent the next few days and nights determined to establish one. And not just to help Jenna, who would be with us before we knew it, but because it was the only thing standing between me and utter chaos.

Being up at 5 a.m. every morning, as now seemed to be the norm, should, in that respect, have been a bit of a bonus. Early birds, or so the proverb goes, catch the worms, after all. But what I hadn't factored in, amid all the frantic plate-spinning, was the extent of the mess; that my usually spotless home would now resemble an art installation – and a very specific one, too. The famous one, by the late 1990s Britart sensation Tracey Emin, descriptively titled 'My Bed'. The bed in question, and the floor around it, being in such a dishevelled state that, even only seeing it reproduced as a photograph, it brought me out in hives. How anyone could ever live like that I didn't know.

But now I did, because my own bed gave hers a run for its money, there being no time to even make it (well, to my standards, though Mike did his best, bless him), much less go back up at any point and tidy and clean the bedroom, as each day began with Seth yelling from across the landing and screaming for his breakfast, duly waking up Tommy, who also started screaming, and me bundling both of them – both howling, the latter damp – downstairs, and the day going downhill from there.

The sense of impending chaos had, by now, become my norm, and I had to fight, much as I had when a young mother myself, not to give into waves of mess-related near-hysteria. Just the sight of my kitchen worktops – usually clear, bar perhaps the occasional vase of flowers – which had become home to all the usual array of baby paraphernalia. Tins of baby formula, steriliser, bottles, brushes, and various bottom creams all remained out, because what point was there in tidying them away, only to get them out again two hours later?

I had also lost my beloved conservatory. Mike had by now spent a couple of evenings repurposing it for Jenna, stopping up the plug sockets with plastic guards, taking out all the house plants, and removing anything else potentially breakable and/or dangerous. Now, as well as the small rattan sofa, armchair, and coffee table which were already in there, there was a single bed, made up ready, a baby-changing unit that Mike had found in a second-hand shop, a wooden swinging crib, for daytime napping (we'd move the big crib downstairs when Jenna came), a large chest of drawers, and a borrowed television. All of which, though it would mean the rest of us were effectively stopped from using it to get out onto the patio, seemed a logical sacrifice to make.

It had been Mike's idea. One much more sensible than cramming the little family into the spare bedroom. 'It makes perfect sense, Case,' he'd explained, being ever-practical. 'This way, she's got plenty of space, she's downstairs, close to the kitchen, for the night feeds, and can just help herself to the bottles from the fridge. Plus, she can bathe the baby there, play with Seth in there, and have direct access to the garden so he can run off some energy – and best of all, it means that, as far as possible, anyway, we have clean, uncluttered space for the rest of us.'

And so I hoped would be the case once Jenna came to join us. Right now, it was just my designated safe child-containment area. And the TV, in particular, had been a godsend. My virtual childminder at least gave me the impression that I had a routine, even if only short-lived: place Tommy in the wooden swinging crib (another charity shop find), put the TV on, sit Seth in front of it by the coffee table, put out a bowl of cereal and carton of juice, quickly make up a bottle, change the baby, make a large cup of coffee while the bottle cooled down, then sit down and feed Tommy in relative peace.

Like all routines, though, mine wasn't completely infallible, as I was to find just six short (*long*) days in.

It was the sort of January morning no one ever wants to wake up to. Dark, for a start – at this time of year, dawn didn't happen for hours yet – and with squally rain that spat aggressively at the conservatory windows every time a gust of wind happened along. No wonder, then, that, after finishing his bottle, Tommy fell deeply back asleep. There wasn't much to be up for, after all. And with Seth so engrossed in the cartoon he was watching, I got it into my head that once I'd put Tommy in the swinging crib, I could snatch another ten or fifteen minutes to do a lightning kitchen clean. The kitchen was connected to the conservatory, after all, and with the door open, I could keep looking in on them.

And for the first ten minutes or so, all was peaceful. I kept checking in every minute or so, soap suds up to my elbows, and once I'd cleared the washing-up and work-tops (well, as much as I was able), I checked back in to see Seth, now finished with his programme, even reaching out from where he was to rock the crib.

In any other circumstance it would have been a case of grab the mobile and catch a cute snap for his mother, so lovely would the image have been to capture. And as soon as he caught my eye, Seth put a finger to his lips. 'Shh,' he then stage-whispered. 'I'm wocking my baby,' before turning his attention back to the opening sequence of the next episode of *PJ Masks* (how many *were* there?).

It was the first time I'd seen Seth show Tommy any affection, and though I knew there were many more hurdles ahead with this complicated little child, it really warmed my heart. It also made me feel guilty about some of the negative feelings I'd continued to have about Seth. He'd had his world turned upside down, after all.

So I nodded, and stepped away again, grabbing a tea towel to dry my hands, so I could make myself another coffee to take back in with me.

What I should have done, however, was remember my own rule. To never leave Seth and Tommy together unattended. Thankfully, though, I didn't make myself that second mug of coffee. Some sixth sense kicked in and it kicked very firmly, reminding me that silence (bar cartoon noise) wasn't always golden. Because when I next popped my head round the door, some thirty seconds later, it was to see something that made me realise that if I *had* made that coffee, the extra two minutes could have been catastrophic.

Seth was now standing over the crib, the TV apparently forgotten, attempting to shovel spoons of soggy cereal into Tommy's mouth, while using his other hand to pinch closed his nose.

'Seth, what on earth are you *doing*?' I barked – well, more shrieked – at him, crossing the space in a single stride and pushing both laden spoon and sticky hands away. Tommy's nose was scarlet, his eyes bulging, his tiny lips stretched, and his little face was a shade of puce I knew all too well. With instinct taking over, I quickly unclipped the restraining straps, and plucked him up so I could tilt his face and torso forwards. It took questing fingers to clear his mouth enough that he could take some precious air in, by which time I was shaking from a jolt of adrenalin the like of which I hadn't felt in years. *Another minute.* A minute more and God only knew what might have happened. 'What were you *doing*?' I snapped at Seth again as I placed Tommy face down against my forearm, reassured, if only slightly, by his lusty, indignant crying. 'He couldn't *breathe*. Didn't you realise? What on earth were you *thinking*?'

Seth crossed his arms and looked up at me defiantly. 'I was *feeding* him.'

But the strange half-smile on his lips went right through me. It was a major wake-up call. I must *never* leave him alone with the baby, I berated myself. Not even for a second. I would need those proverbial eyes in the back of my head, and so would Jenna, clearly. Which thought, and idea, with its demonic connotations, couldn't help but go through me as well.

I watched the pair of them like a hawk for the rest of the day, obviously, and by the end of it, when nothing else untoward happened, I calmed down a bit. Perhaps he was just trying to be helpful. And when Tyler returned home from his trip later in the day, Seth was sweetness personified, eager to see the bedroom that had so far been off-limits to him, and marvelling that Tyler had not one but two computer monitors (modern life, eh?), and full of questions about the games he liked to play.

In other circumstances I'd have looked upon it all as a positive. Perhaps a natural bond would form between them – Tyler was always good with little ones – and it would help with the inevitable shift in dynamic once his mum was installed and things changed once again. But I couldn't get Seth's expression out of my mind, even when I was gifted another cuddle when I put him to bed. In fact, I was wondering – was this four-year-old playing me?

'I think we need to give him the benefit of the doubt, love,' was Mike's considered opinion when I shared my feeling with him over tea. It was just the two of us and Tommy, currently sleeping in his baby seat on the floor beside me, as, having returned, Tyler was getting ready to go out again. Some sort of end-of-trip get-together at the local pub.

'I keep thinking that,' I said, 'but just the expression on his face … you'd have to see it to understand, I suppose, but it really got to me.'

'But he's *four*. Can kids of four even *have* murderous intentions?'

'I don't know, I don't *think* so. But he just seemed so malevolent.'

'Which toddlers can. Remember Kieron with that hammer-the-coloured-balls-into-the-holes thing he had? He could wield that thing like bloody Thor when he didn't get his way.'

Mike was right. I'd even had to take him out of play group on one occasion – him screaming blue murder and my face as red as the weal on the unfortunate friend's head. But this felt different. And, at four, Seth was no longer a toddler. And he hadn't been lashing out. He'd been calmly pinching his little brother's nose in such a way that it made it impossible for him to breathe.

And I was just about to point that out when we heard the doorbell.

'I'll get it,' I said, expecting Tyler's friend Denver. He'd just passed his driving test and was now the proud owner of an elderly blue hatchback. Which development seemed nigh-on impossible. It seemed like only ten minutes since he and Tyler were ten. How was it that life seemed to whoosh by so fast?

I was about to get another wake-up call in that regard, too. Because I opened the door not to Denver, but a pretty young female. Skinny jeans, suede jacket, black polo-neck, glossy bob.

'Hi,' she said, smiling shyly. 'I'm Naomi. Here for Tyler?' Then glanced back, to where Denver's car was, indeed, parked, across the road.

'Hi,' I began. 'He's –'

'Coming!' he finished for me, as he clattered down the stairs, grabbing his own jacket from the newel post as he did so, without breaking stride, as if appearing in a scene in a sit-com. The air was thick with aftershave. I looked from one to the other. I wasn't sure which of them was blushing more profusely.

I know that kind of blush, I thought. *That's a very specific kind of blush*. 'Casey,' I said. 'Nice to meet you.'

'Same!' the girl trilled. And was, I think, about to say more, were it not for the fact that she was already being ushered back off the doorstep by my son.

'Gotta go. Don't wait up, Mum, okay?' Tyler ordered, glancing back, briefly and self-consciously, as he bundled her down the front path.

'No danger of that!' I said, but they were already out of earshot.

I went back into the dining room, where Mike was just clearing the plates, all thoughts of Seth now buried beneath another.

'Hmm. I suspect we have a girlfriend,' I announced.

Chapter 7

Naomi was, of course, big family news. So I was dying to meet up with Riley, now also back from Lanzarote. But I couldn't see how it was possible now that I had the two little ones to take care of, and especially given how on pins I felt about Seth. There was no way I could ask Riley to bring the kids around, not with him being as he was, and the same applied to me going round to hers. Which was frustrating, as I was looking forward to hearing all about her time in the sun, but also wanted to pass on all the gossip about Tyler having a girlfriend. Well, that he was 'seeing her', a fact I had managed to ascertain before he'd left for football, and, in my defence, under only very slight duress.

I was also by now missing some cuddles with our newest grandson, Carter, so was keen to see Lauren as well. But how? Happily, Mike, highly amused by my reaction to 'fully grown man is in romantic relationship', suggested a plan to kill all of those birds with one stone.

'I'll take Seth out for a couple of hours,' he said. 'We'll go and watch the lads having a kick-about, and then I can take him across to the park, expend a bit of that energy he has, and it'll give me a chance to have a little chat with him about what he did to Tommy. You never know, he might just open up a bit under different circumstances.'

'You sure, love?' I asked, though the question was rhetorical – I was already reaching for my mobile. 'Only I'll ring the girls right now and see if they want to meet up at that new coffee place in the precinct.'

Mike laughed. 'Best take my credit card too, then, if you're going to that bloody Costafortune! And yes, I'm sure, but you'll have to take the baby along.'

Well, of *course* I was taking the baby along. Not only did I not want to put too much on Mike, but I also wanted to show off this gorgeous bundle to my daughter and unofficial daughter-in-law. They both loved babies, and I figured that while they were passing him about and cooing over him, I could do the same with my latest little grandson, who I'd only seen on FaceTime for over a week. So, the second that Mike and a very disgruntled Seth left the house, I was stowing the neat blue pram social services had delivered to me into the boot of the car, strapping in the baby seat, and heading off into town, feeling as giddy with freedom as if I'd just been let out of prison.

Lattes and frap-a-something-or-others ordered, and babies jiggling on our knees, we were soon engrossed in what we did best – a mile-a-minute gossip and catch-up. Thankfully, Lauren had already filled Riley in with the details of our latest placement, so I could skip all that, mostly, and get to the good part.

'So, did either of you know about Tyler's new girl-friend?' I asked.

Riley shook her head, but I noticed Lauren didn't.

I raised my eyebrows enquiringly.

'Not till last night,' she added quickly. 'Honestly, or I'd have mentioned it. I literally only found out because Kieron bumped into them in the pub and Ty told him it was okay to go public.'

'Go public? What are they, the royal family or something?'

Riley rolled her eyes. 'Mum, you are priceless, you know that?'

'He just didn't want anyone knowing till they were official,' Lauren added. 'That's all. Kieron only knew because he knows her. And Ty swore him to secrecy. Which is –'

'I see I shall have to have words – keeping secrets from their own mother! And what's "official" mean? Did she have to pass some sort of test?'

Now Riley burst out laughing. 'Mum, official just means official. As in they update their social media profiles and –'

'*What*? We're his family. Do we play second fiddle to Facebook?'

Lauren grinned. 'No! Which is why he didn't want to say anything,' she explained. 'In case it didn't *come* to anything.'

'Mum, get over yourself, seriously,' Riley added, still grinning.

'I have,' I huffed, and in truth I wasn't actually in a huff. Just intrigued. 'Anyway, spill then,' I said. 'What's she like?'

'Mother!' Riley spluttered now, as Lauren coloured. 'Lauren just *told* you, she only found out herself last night. God, no wonder our Tyler was keeping her under wraps for a bit.'

Now it was my turn to blush. 'Oh, you know me. I only meant …'

'It's okay, Casey,' Lauren said. 'And as it happens, I do know her a bit. I mean, not now, it was a couple of years ago. She was actually one of my dance students, with me for about four months.'

This was just the kind of juicy insider knowledge I'd been hoping for. Carter was asleep now, so I placed him back in his buggy, all the better to concentrate. 'And?' I urged as I picked up my coffee. 'What was she like?'

A bit of a 'princess', by the sound of it. At least back then. Lauren explained that although all the other dancers turned up to class fresh-faced, hair tied back and ready to do some serious work, Naomi usually arrived looking like she'd just stepped out of a beauty salon. Hair curled to perfection and a full face of impeccable make-up. 'She left looking exactly the same too,' Lauren said. 'Not a hair out of place, and not a bit of sweat on her designer dancewear. I'm not sure dancing was really her thing, to be honest.'

I let that process as my mind conjured up a TV-style, American cheerleader-type with a beaming, white smile and perfectly manicured nails. Which, to be fair, was not how she'd seemed the night before. 'Okay, but what was she like as a *person*?'

'Mother!' Riley admonished. 'Stop digging! Were you like this when I got with David? And when Lauren got with our Kieron?'

'Well, of *course* I was,' I said, a tad defensively. 'It's my job! This is Tyler's first serious girlfriend, don't forget. I don't want him heartbroken, do I? I need to establish her credentials!'

'Leave him *be*, Mum,' Riley said, with her stern face in place.

We had a lovely catch-up, despite the girls teasing me about my detective skills. Which was fair enough, I supposed. They must have thought I was mad, practically demanding a background check – I mean, I had met the girl and she'd seemed perfectly lovely. I knew I was just naturally over-protective of Tyler; after all he'd been through in his early childhood, he was understandably a late developer, his self-esteem, despite his good looks and confident-seeming ways, still a fragile thing. But he was also an adult now, old enough to make his own decisions. And any meddling from me wouldn't prevent the almost inevitable heartbreak that came from 'first love', no matter how much I tried to prevent it. Time to step back and loosen the apron strings.

And right now I had my own life to be getting on with, which would no doubt require all my energies over the coming few weeks. And while my free time had passed all too quickly and pleasantly, I had a feeling that Mike's would have seemed like an eternity. As I drove down our road, still smiling to myself about Tyler having a 'proper' girlfriend, a glance in my rear-view mirror revealed I was probably right. Mike was crossing the road, back at the corner I'd just driven past, marching in resolute fashion, face set like stone, and carrying a kicking Seth under one arm.

Rather than wait in the cold, I unbuckled Tommy's car seat and took him inside, leaving the front door open for my stony-faced husband.

'Come on, Baby,' I whispered, 'let's get you out of the way before your big brother comes in and upsets you.'

I had already given Tommy his bottle at the coffee shop, so luckily he was ready to finish off the doze he'd already started in the car. I tucked him into his conservatory Moses basket, turned on the musical teddy bear that sat on a table beside him, and then went back into the hall to see what had happened.

Mike shook his head, though, and walked past me, straight up the stairs, seemingly impervious to the kicking, writhing bundle he was carrying.

'Casey!' Seth shouted, as soon as he saw me. 'Get him off me! He's a bastard! Make him put me down!'

'Hush now,' I said, 'and stop kicking like that!'

Upon which, he cranked his neck round and spat towards my face. 'You're a bitch!' he raved. 'Biiiitttchhh!'

'Enough!' Mike barked. 'You hear me?'

I trailed on up the stairs, and, sensing Mike wanted to deal with this one solo, hovered on the landing just outside Seth's bedroom door.

'You *knew* what was going to happen,' he said, while Seth continued ranting. 'You were given the chance to say sorry and be a good boy, but you didn't want to. Which means it's now time out in your room, like I told you. End of.'

He then backed out of the room, closing the door behind him, and holding on tightly to the handle. Almost immediately came the sound of Seth booting the door, which went on for a minute, along with further shouting and sobbing, before it finally began subsiding and eventually stopped.

'Ten minutes,' Mike said, 'then I will come back and fetch you down. And if you come down before that, I shall bring you back up again. And again, for as long as I need to. Jesus, Case,' he muttered, as we headed back downstairs, 'that boy's a bloody nightmare!'

'Coffee?' I suggested as we went into the kitchen.

'Please,' he said. '*God*, I could use a double whiskey.'

His expression was so grim I thought he might even have meant it. Despite the fact that it wasn't even one in the afternoon yet. Despite the fact that he didn't even drink whiskey.

'That bad, huh?' I said.

'That bad. Seriously, the boy's a force of nature. As in a bad one. Like a monster tornado.'

There had, it seemed, been a fracas in the park. Seth had climbed to the top of the slide and, as kids sometimes do, had decided he didn't want to slide down it. Not in a scared way, Mike thought. Just an 'I've changed my mind' way, specifically, it appeared, just to annoy the queue of kids forming on the steps behind him. And when a bigger boy, next up, had leaned in to try and persuade him, Seth had punched the boy's nose, almost toppling him off the steps and causing a nosebleed, to boot.

'So there I am,' he said, 'trying to slither up the slide to grab his ankle, while the boy at the top is up there clutching his nose and sobbing, and the girl behind him is screaming at the top of her lungs, and the little lad behind her tries to go back down the steps, misses his footing, and falls the rest of the way, and –'

'Oh, God, was he hurt?'

'No. It was only three steps and he got straight back up, but, of course, parents are rushing up, and when I do get hold of Seth, he's kicking out so much that I get a boot in the eye.' He touched his eye socket. 'I'll probably have a shiner there tomorrow.'

'Oh dear,' I began, reaching for mugs.

'That's not all. I'm heading round to check the other kids are okay, with Seth over my shoulder, of course, when this young guy runs up – not sure whose dad he was – and tells me I deserve a punch on my own nose for bringing such a "little shit" to the park in the first place, just to see how *I'd* like it. I mean, seriously? So, of course, I try to calm Seth down enough to extract an apology, but there's as much chance of that happening as pigs flying, obviously, so all I can do is apologise and make a break for it, and the whole way – the *whole* way, past genteel couples and little old ladies out walking their dogs – he's screaming C-U-N-T, repeatedly, over and over. I'm not sure I'll ever be able to show my face in there again.'

He painted such a picture, a part of me almost laughed. Except it wasn't funny, and I could see his eye was already swelling.

'You'll need some peas on that,' I began, but he hadn't quite finished.

'Oh, and he's going to burn our "fucking house down". He told me that just as I was passing old Mr Hughes at number seven. He's not safe in public, love. He really isn't.'

The kettle boiled then. 'I guess we just have to hope that things change when his mum arrives. This is all down to that, I'm sure. He's raging. He's lost.'

'Easy for you to say, fresh from your overpriced coffee break.' But he smiled as he said that, even though I already knew he didn't mean it. 'Anyway, is ten minutes up yet? I think I'd better go and bring him down again. God knows what he'll be getting up to up there.'

'Must be,' I said. 'I'll go and fetch the bag of peas out. And you never know, he might have calmed down enough to apologise now.'

Wishful thinking. Because no sooner had Mike gone upstairs than he was calling me to come up as well, to find the bedroom, perhaps predictably, in chaos. Seth himself was sitting cross-legged on his bed, as if butter wouldn't melt, watching a cartoon on the TV. Around him it looked like a war zone. Every single stuffed toy had been pulled apart – heads ripped off, arms and legs dismembered, fluff everywhere, and the half-dozen jigsaws I should have removed but hadn't had been tipped all over the floor – all stirred together and unlikely to ever be sorted.

Worse than all of that, though, was that Seth had obviously taken down his pants, and gone to the toilet on the carpet. The smell was horrendous. He smiled as I appeared, gagging, in the doorway.

'Sorry,' he said sweetly, 'but I needed a poo. And I'm sorry about that kid at the park, Mike.' He listened then, as did we, to a wail from below. 'You better see to the baby now,' he told me dismissively.

Chapter 8

A week or so later – maybe more, I couldn't be sure as the days had begun running into each other now – I was fending off a very hyper Seth in the kitchen, when my phone rang.

'Stop it, Seth!' I warned, raising my voice, 'and put that rolling pin down, please. You will hurt yourself swinging it round like that.'

Or me, I thought, rubbing my side and spreading flour all over my black jeggings as I answered my mobile with a dusty hand.

'Gilly Collins,' the female caller said. 'I don't think we've spoken before, but I'm Sam Burdett's manager.'

'Oh, hello,' I said, still a bit breathless from trying to wrestle the rolling pin back that Seth had snatched during what was meant to be a jolly baking session. 'Sorry, you've caught me at a busy time,' I continued. 'Mind you, any time is a busy time just lately.'

Gilly laughed. As she would. Because she wasn't living it. 'I bet it is,' she said, as Seth and I played tug of war with the rolling pin, 'and I'm sorry to disturb you, but I thought you'd want to be the first to know the news.'

I leapt at this, perhaps the nursery place had been organised? Though with the events of two weeks back I had to temper my hope – how long would a nursery keep him, after all, given how unpredictable and violent Seth's behaviour was?

Not that I'd been tempted to test it. Since Mike's adventures with him in the park, I had avoided it altogether. Much as I'd been keen to escape the house, being on my own with the two of them meant not enough hands and arms to restrain him – if he kicked off while I was pushing the baby in the pram, I was too anxious that I could quickly lose control of him. And there was no way I would attempt to put a toddler 'lead' on him. It felt too much like asking for even more trouble; I had to clear a vision of having to drag him along the street with it. So home it would be, for the most part, at least – Mike 'spelling' me for a precious hour or two at the end of each day, so I could go to the shops, or pop to Riley's or Lauren's for a coffee. But, apart from that and, the previous weekend, Tyler and Naomi taking him to the woods for an hour (about which I'd fretted – what on earth would she make of him? Or him her, for that matter?), it was very much a case of little person-wrangling, solo. So a few free hours a week would be a very welcome gift, both now and when his mother arrived.

Which it seemed she was about to. Gilly Collins, it seemed, wasn't calling about a nursery place. 'We've been told we can collect Jenna this morning,' she told me, 'so hopefully we will get to yours later this afternoon.'

An even bigger weight immediately lifted from my shoulders. 'Oh,' I said. 'How come? I though she wasn't due for another week yet.'

'It's because of her six-week post-natal check,' she explained. 'We've already registered her with your local GP, and I think the decision was made that it would be best to let her out so she can attend it, since she's being released into your care anyway, and achieve some continuity with her and the baby's post-natal healthcare. Plus, her release date falls on a Sunday, so she'd have been going early anyway. All just logistics. And paperwork. And perhaps they need her bed. The main point is that we can bring her to you sometime this afternoon. Does that work for you?'

'Of course. Yes, that's fine ... ouch! Hang on,' I said, as Seth, having jerked the rolling pin out of my floury hand, whacked me across the leg with it.

'Are you okay?'

'Hang on,' I said again, putting the mobile on the counter, and setting off around the table to catch him. 'Seth! Put that *down*,' I demanded once I got him cornered. 'You're not in trouble if you put it back now, but if you don't, then the baking stops and the pastry goes in the bin, and then, also, what will happen at 3 o'clock? Remember?'

'No *PJ Masks*, no TV,' Seth trotted out – proving that he at least knew the drill now.

'That's right,' I confirmed. 'So what are you going to do? It's up to you.'

Seth threw the rolling pin across the kitchen, narrowly missing my legs again. However, much as I would have liked to tell him off for that action, I couldn't. Mike and I had fast learned that any tiny compliance, no matter how it was achieved, was still a compliance, and for now we had to ignore the manner in which he chose to make the right choice.

'Good boy,' I said, forcing a smile I wasn't feeling. 'Now if you will just sit nicely at the table while I finish talking on the phone, we will get straight back to making your jam tarts. Okay? Perhaps you could build me a nice tower out of your bricks.'

Seth glared at me – he seemed to genuinely hate doing anything deemed as 'good' or 'nice'. 'Not a tower, I'll build a wrecking machine, and then kill all the stupid figures.'

I picked the phone back up again while Seth lined up the poor *PJ Masks* figures that Mike had bought him the week before. Little Owlette and the crew had no idea they were about to be violently abused.

'Sorry about that,' I told Gilly, once I stepped just outside the kitchen door. 'It's so difficult to give anyone else my attention when Seth's around. Thank goodness Tommy is such a poppet. I don't know how we'd have coped if he'd been a needy baby. Anyway, sorry, go on. This afternoon, you say?'

'Yes. If you're sure you can talk? You really do sound as if your hands are full and then some.'

'No, it's fine. What sort of time?'

'Around four, if all is well. It's been a little touch-and-go – she's terribly nervous about coming to you. At one point they were talking about her going back to her parents –'

'What, as in giving up the children?'

'No, just to reorient herself a little. Spend a few days there first, before entering the fray, so to speak.'

Something that wouldn't, I thought, strengthen her case any. Young and scared though she might be, this whole process was predicated on her wanting to prove she was committing to do exactly that, however hard it might be. Putting off the moment when she stepped in and took responsibility for her babies would not make for the best first impression. Not least because it would hardly make it look as if she was desperate to be with them again, would it? 'But she's okay now?' I asked, wondering if her stay with us might end up being more short-lived than planned, the ramifications of which I didn't even want to think about.

'Absolutely,' Gilly said. 'Just a case of the wobbles, which I think is to be expected. She's okay about it now, having spoken at length to her prison counsellor, but she's bound to feel a bit awkward, having to jump straight back into taking care of her children under the scrutiny of complete strangers.'

Which was exactly what we were, I reflected, as I

reassured Gilly that we'd do everything we could to make the transition easy for her. It didn't matter how much we tried to put her at ease, though. It would be a daunting prospect for anyone, let alone someone so young and vulnerable, and who'd been through so much. I knew barely anything about this girl but I couldn't – didn't – blame her for the pickle she was in. One thing long experience made me pretty certain of was that a combination of poor, haphazard parenting and substance abuse were almost certainly the twin architects of the place she resided in right now, and I didn't doubt her 'crime' (given her short sentence and the fact that they seemed happy to let her out early) was probably in service of some bigger, badder dealer. I could only hope that seeing her children again would put her in a better place. Put us *all* in one, her oldest son included.

Her son who, right now, was giving a proper pasting to a bunch of plastic figures, and put me in mind of the boy in the second *Toy Story* movie – Sid, was it? – who routinely tortured his toys. Breaking the cycle was the thing. The only answer.

'Why are they called jam tarts?' Seth wanted to know, once we resumed the aborted baking session. 'My grandad says my mum's a tart,' he added conversationally.

Despite my checking the clock every twenty minutes or so for the rest of the day, by teatime there was still no word from anyone. First, Tyler came home from work, starving, and then Mike, also starving, which meant both of them sulking when I told them I couldn't dish up because Jenna might arrive at any moment.

I bathed and fed Baby Tommy and dressed him up in a cute little outfit I'd found in his belongings – his mummy would love to see him dressed like a tiny sailor, I was sure of it. Then I attempted to give Seth his tea. He had definitely asked for noodles and bread, but now as I served it up, he was kicking off as well.

'I hate noodles!' he yelled angrily, 'I didn't say noodles, I said bacon and egg!'

'No you did not,' I replied in a calm voice. 'Now sit down nicely please and eat your tea.'

The noodles and dish they were in suddenly went flying past my ear before crashing down all over the kitchen floor.

'Oh my God, Mum,' Tyler said, hopping out of the way just in time to avoid having his best going-out shirt almost splattered with noodle juice. (A shirt, I noted, that had been on two outings already this week.) 'This is ridiculous!' He leaned in towards Seth. 'That's *very* naughty,' he admonished him. 'Now, what do you say to Casey?'

'Fuck off!' Seth yelled right in Tyler's face. '*You* eat the scabby noodles!'

'Yeah, right. Off the *floor*?' Tyler huffed at him.

The baby's Moses basket had been brought into the dining room so he was there right away when his mummy walked in, so I knew it was safe to do what I did next.

'Right,' I said, my nerves jangling. 'Come on, young man,' I said, putting a hand out for him to take as I approached the kitchen table. 'Time out in your mummy's new room for you.'

Seth clambered into a squatting position on the chair and, eyes wild, started to kick out at me. 'Fuck off!' he screamed. 'Get away from me right now, you slag!'

Not willing to stand down at this stage in the day, but also mindful that Jenna was due to turn up any moment, I didn't want too much fuss. So, ignoring the hard kicks to my stomach, I reached under his armpits and picked him up. I hadn't counted on the hair pulling that followed, but I endured it as I made my way into the conservatory.

Mike followed and, as I lay the kicking child down on the little sofa, kindly unclasped his fingers from the clumps of my hair that Seth decided to hang onto for grim death.

'Quick,' I said to Mike, nodding towards the door. We needed to make our exit before Seth had the chance to wriggle up and run past us. I then stood in the open doorway, bodily guarding the gap.

'No!' I said, as he did exactly that. 'Go and sit back down for two minutes, please. Your mummy will be here very soon and what do you think she will say if she sees you behaving like this?'

'Don't *care* what she says,' he shouted. 'She's a fat, junkie slag!'

It didn't matter how many times I heard such language, I remained shocked that he would call his mother these names. It was obvious he had heard them from someone – but who? His grandparents? Some boyfriend? Whoever it had been, they had certainly made an impression on Seth's young brain.

'Shout and yell as much as you like,' I said. 'We won't listen to you until you calm down and be sensible.' I turned away then, to where Mike and Tyler were both looking on with the same exasperated expressions, and purposely lifted my voice to almost sing-song level. 'Hey, you guys,' I trilled, 'why don't you help yourselves to the casserole? The dumplings should be done now, so go and dig in. Save some for Jenna though, because she's bound to want some when she gets here, and if Seth is still acting out, he'll be in here with me, so let her know she can see him after her tea.'

Of course, I wouldn't have dreamed of keeping Seth from his mother – she would be reunited with him the very minute she walked in, obviously. But at least the threat seemed to work.

'Fine,' he growled, glowering at me as he stepped back from the conservatory doorway. 'Eat your castle-ole. I don't care. I'm tired anyway, so I'm going to have a lie-down. On the floor.'

I hid the smile that threatened to give me away when I heard the 'on the floor' bit. I knew it was just a case of Seth feeling he'd retained a little control. He wasn't about to lie down anywhere that he knew I'd have liked him to. Still, right now, it suited me just fine.

'Well, okay then,' I said. 'In that case, I might just go

get some tea for myself and then come back to see you in five minutes.' Then I walked away before he had the chance to swear at me.

Which he didn't. In itself a tiny increment of progress. But what about when Mum came, as was due to happen any time now? I would have to step back then. That was what I'd signed up for. Would such progress as we had made all come undone?

Chapter 9

Normally, by 7 p.m. we were starting the process of putting Seth to bed. Mike would play with the baby, while I went through the arduous routine of standing outside Seth's bedroom, listening to him jump straight out of bed, leaving it for a minute, then going in and putting him back to bed again. This went on for at least half an hour, with various tactics used to keep him there, and often resulted in something being smashed or torn apart, but Seth would eventually get tired and go to sleep.

Tonight though, we couldn't do that. Sam Burdett had phoned at 6 p.m. to apologise for the hold-up, but promised that they would be with us within the hour.

'Jenna's led us a bit of a merry dance,' he explained, sounding tetchy, 'but she's in Gilly's car now, and we're on our way.'

By now I was super-stressed, and in no mood for pointless placations. 'At half past four,' I pointed out,

'Gilly phoned to say you guys were on your way. Seth is difficult enough at the best of times, but when he's over-tired, it's ten times worse. What's the hold-up?'

Sam had the grace to sound a bit sheepish. 'I'm sorry, Casey,' he said, 'but we had to take Jenna to her flat first, because she told us she had to pick up some things for the children. Anyway, turned out that was just a ruse and all the kids' things were actually at her parents. She spent a bloody hour and a half at her own flat, putting together a collection of hair products, straighteners, earrings, make-up – you name it. So we've only just left her parents now – they live right on the other side of town. Plus, we caught the rush hour, of course. Like I said, I'm so sorry, but we genuinely are on our way now.'

I allowed myself a small smile at this piece of decep-tion. Probably necessary, in Jenna's mind – these things might not matter to a man, but to a young girl, especially one newly free from incarceration, they probably seemed of utmost importance. Still, it would probably have been better to come clean in the first place.

'Okay,' I said, 'well, we obviously can't put Seth to bed then. He knows his mum is coming, so we'll just have to try our best to keep him occupied – not to mention awake.'

After another hour of feeding and changing the baby while Mike literally ran around the house retrieving Seth from one room or another (Tyler having beat a hasty retreat to meet Naomi as soon as he'd wolfed down his tea), we heard the two cars finally pull up outside, and, having scooped Seth up onto my hip, now all shy excitement, went for the obligatory look out of the window. It was a dark, moonless night, so I couldn't really see who was who, but the young girl's silhouetted form was unmistakable. 'Guess who's here?' I said to Seth. 'Come on, let's meet her at the door.'

It was a hearteningly textbook reunion. 'Mummy!' Seth cried out, as Jenna, flanked by both Sam and Gilly, walked towards us, long blonde hair being lifted in skeins by the chilly breeze. He wriggled down from my arms and ran to her, arms wide. 'Mummy!' he said, wrapping both arms around her thighs. 'Can we go home?' he asked, despite us telling him multiple times that this wasn't what was going to be happening. 'We can leave Baby here. It's got its own room and its bum stinks. I don't want it at ours.'

I watched with interest at this unlikely but, at a deeper level, perhaps only natural exchange. Hadn't Riley said almost as much when I brought Kieron home from hospital? That he was boring, and cried all the time, and could we just send him back again?

More arresting, however, was the sight of the girl herself. She might be down on record as being nineteen, but could easily have passed for fourteen or fifteen. There was so little of her she looked as if a strong wind could blow not just her hair but the rest of her away. She also looked tired, undernourished, and way too small for the long teddy-bear coat she was swaddled in, her wrists sprung from the arms like two twigs.

Despite her apparent frailty, however, she had no trouble scooping up her son with her strong, young person's arms. Holding him up and out so she could look him in the eyes, she planted a kiss on her forehead before speaking.

'I've missed you, my beautiful boy,' she whispered. 'So, *so* much. And, oh, where's all your beautiful hair?'

'Nanna shaved it off with Gramp's clippers,' he told her. 'She said I'd have nits again if she didn't. Can we go now? We don't need to take the baby. It's fine for him to stay here.'

'But he's your brother! And don't say nasty things about him, you little monkey. Anyway, did you miss me?'

Seth nodded an affirmative. 'You smell nice,' he said. 'Can we go now? Can we please? The lady can drive us.'

This needed nipping in the bud. 'Come on in,' I said, smiling. 'It's freezing out there. Let's get back in the warm. And I think little Tommy is still awake – I'm sure you'd love a cuddle all together. Seth, why don't you take Mummy straight through to him in the kitchen? Seth's been helping me look after him,' I added. 'He's *such* a good big brother.'

Outrageous hype – indeed, probably actionable by the advertising standards authority, but it felt important to put Seth in a place where he *felt* important.

Jenna looked beyond me, then, to the door, where Mike was standing, filling the space. To a young trauma-tised teen, another hurdle to be jumped. A big male stranger, in whose house she was going to be residing. No wonder she was anxious.

She seemed to struggle to make eye contact, but eventually met my smiling gaze. 'Thank you,' she said, 'but do you mind if I use your loo first? I've been needing a pee since we set off.'

Seth wouldn't be put down, so she carried him over the threshold and, since there was no danger of him letting go of her, took him into the downstairs loo with her, leaving Gilly and Sam to follow her into the house and shrug their coats off. I took them into the dining room, to get comfortable at the table, since they'd be here a little while to deal with all the paperwork.

'Absolutely freezing out there,' Sam said, rubbing his arms briskly, then cupping his hands and breathing into them.

'Coffee?' I suggested.

'Music to my ears,' he said. 'If it's not any trouble, that is. Or would you rather get on?' he added, glancing at Gilly.

'I'd love a coffee,' Gilly added. 'I've not had a drop of anything since I left the office for the prison. Just a quick one, if it isn't too much trouble.'

'On it,' said Mike, heading off into the kitchen.

I was surprised, though. 'You mean we don't have to go through reams of paperwork and care plans and so on?'

Gilly shook her head. 'There's no care plan for Jenna, since you're not technically fostering her. But we do need to quickly go through the agreement we've made up for her. Just a document laying out our expectations for the placement. For Jenna, but also for you and Mike. Just a couple of pages, which we've obviously already run through with her, so really it's just for you guys to read through and agree to.'

It was very different from the last mother and baby placement I'd had. In that one, I'd been fostering both the baby *and* the fourteen-year-old mum, and when she disclosed that she was pregnant again, she was already in situ.

Sam was just opening the sheets out when Jenna came back, by way of the kitchen, apparently, because she now had the baby in the crook of her arm. She was still in her coat, though. Perhaps it felt like some kind of armour. Perhaps she too was toying with the possibility of going home. It must have been strange, after all, to have gone to her flat, knowing her own home was the one place she *couldn't* go. Seth, gazing up at her, was holding on tightly to her other hand. It looked like a scene from a happy maternity poster, rather than one of a fractured family, potentially on the brink of complete breakdown.

Gilly looked up and smiled. 'Come join us for a few minutes, Jenna,' she said. 'It's okay, you can bring Tommy. I know you've missed him.'

Jenna looked a little uncertain, as she would do, but Mike pulled out a chair for her, and soon we were all clustered round as if to start a card game – an impression enhanced as Sam passed out paper-clipped copies of 'the agreement' to each of us.

'Now,' he said, 'as Gilly mentioned, it's pretty straight-forward and, as you can see, Jenna has already agreed and signed each copy, so if you scan through it, Casey, and put your signature on there, that's really all we have to do tonight. I'll be leaving each of you a copy, so you can read through it again at your leisure.'

I started to read, first an overview, then the meat of what my job was going to be from now on, my heart starting to sink with each new edict I read, each politely set out for me with a neat bullet point.

Jenna must NOT be left in the home unsupervised.

Jenna must NOT leave the home with her children, unsupervised.

Jenna must NOT be left unsupervised with her children.

Jenna MUST smoke in the garden with all house doors closed, and then wash her hands on re-entry to the house.

Jenna must NOT contact any friends from her past.

Jenna must NOT drink any alcohol.

Jenna must NOT take Baby to any appointments without supervision.

Jenna CANNOT attend any contact visits set up for the children.

Well, that was just a snippet from the 'straightforward' two-page document. It made for dire reading and although I felt instantly sorry for Jenna as I watched her reddening face – it made her appear to be a monster who might hurt her babies – I also felt sick for myself. Yes, I'd known what we were getting into, and hadn't underestimated how exacting the rules were likely to be, but seeing them set down like this – all those must-nots – brought it suddenly into much starker focus. I was already stuck at home to a far greater extent than I was used to, but the situation was compounded now by the enormity of the logistics.

When Mike and Tyler were at work I couldn't leave the house without dragging all three of them with me, and at no point could Jenna have even the smallest bit of freedom with her own babies. She couldn't so much as take them for a walk round the block, not without me in tow as well. For as long as this lasted we would be completely bound together, both inside the home and out of it. Her only freedom, in fact, was to go out without them. Which she obviously was free to do – I held no jurisdiction over her – and I wondered how long, given how on top of one another we'd be, it would be before she was tempted to do exactly that. Young children were stressful, even for the most committed mother. It was a big ask for such a young, troubled girl.

'I'm sorry if I look a little shocked,' I said, aware that everyone was staring at me, 'it's just I didn't realise the placement would be so fully supervised.' I removed my reading glasses and looked at Jenna in sympathy. 'According to this, there's very little Jenna can do with the children without me tagging along. Is that right?'

Sam and Gilly nodded in unison. 'I'm sorry,' Gilly said. 'I thought your supervising social worker would have explained that. As Jenna knows, the original plan was for her to go home from prison and the two children into foster care, while she applied through the courts to get them back. The judge has only agreed to Jenna's request to remain with them on the express condition that it's in a closely supervised setting such as this one. I know it sounds onerous, but I think we all accept why it's necessary, and if everyone plays their part …' she looked again at Jenna, '… there is a good chance – a fighting chance – that this will work out.'

As long as I played my part, which I was suddenly thinking I perhaps shouldn't have been quite so quick to audition for. Yet the young girl sitting across my dining table was looking at me too now. Blue eyes assessing me from under a lank fringe. Thinking what? I couldn't tell. Did *she* think she could do this? I had to believe so –

that failure wasn't a foregone conclusion, even knowing what I knew about her background, and that of her eldest child. To think anything different would be just too depressing.

And why was I surprised? Didn't I actually already know all this? Had I been so keen to take this family on that I'd allowed my brain to skip over the technicalities? Let heart rule head?

'She did explain,' I said, loyal to Christine, because I *had* known what I was doing. 'Knowing me, perhaps I didn't take it all in properly. Anyway, here we are,' I added, picking up Sam's proffered pen. I smiled at the girl. 'You can do this, Jenna.'

Then I scribbled my illegible signature on all the copies, knowing that I really was signing away life as I knew it.

Chapter 10

The first big change after Jenna moved in was that I had to accept that 'my home, my rules' no longer applied in a normal sense. Where I had thought giving Jenna her own mother and baby space might allow a return to some normality in my usually tidy home, it seemed the temporary baby station in the kitchen was to become a permanent feature, the previous clutter only added to by an even larger sterilising unit and even more baby paraphernalia, which was creeping in daily, despite my having moved everything wholesale into her area. When I pointed this out, Jenna simply smiled and shook her head, as if I was asking the incomprehensible. 'Oh, it makes much more sense for me to have everything in the kitchen,' she'd explained, as if I'd had a total logic bypass. 'It's crazy for me to be going back and forth washing bottles and taking them back into the conservatory all the time.'

Yes, I thought, *but that's not the point.*

But I stopped short of pointing it out to her, as to do so would be like saying she wasn't part of the family –

more like a lodger – which was not the message I wanted or should be putting out. She had to feel I was behind her – even as my job was to judge her – because without my support, she could all too easily lose motivation once the reality of looking after two little ones kicked in.

It was a small detail, however, and I needed to get over myself – just as I needed to try not to mind that, at a stroke, wherever I stepped there were now toys underfoot, since I must not now run around tidying up for her. Yes, I could suggest that she might like to make a game with Seth called 'tidying up' but to go further would be too much like directing her.

The brutal truth was that, for the first time in my professional life, I had no control over the children *I* was fostering. I *was* both Seth and Tommy's foster carer – the buck stopped with me, I knew that – but Jenna was there too now, and she was their mother, so mother them she must. I could only step in if I thought there was a safeguarding issue. *All* the mothering, therefore, had to be done by her. The problem was that she was expected to mother them under the scrutiny of another mother, and I had to allow her to look after her children as though she were in her own home with them. That meant cooking, feeding, bathing and, when required, in Seth's case, tellings-off. I was used to doing all of those things, obviously, had done them for years, but I soon learned that Jenna's methods were miles from my own. Forget the small differences in method with, say, my grandchildren; Jenna's methods were light years away.

'Go away, you little shit!' I heard her bark at Seth on only the third day she was with us. 'I mean it, just piss off, I'm on the phone.'

Here was an aspect I could at least pass comment on. Rushing to her makeshift downstairs bedroom, I knocked and then opened the door. 'Love,' I said, '*please*, I wish you wouldn't speak to Seth like that. This is why we're struggling to get him not to swear.'

It wasn't the first time she had spoken to her son using that sort of language, but she looked at me as though I were speaking in a foreign one.

'Like what?' she asked, looking genuinely puzzled. 'He can see I'm on the phone to my mate. We haven't spoken for months and he's doing my head in!'

So, no mention of her language at all. I noticed that Baby seemed settled in his basket and that he seemed to be enjoying the fact that his mum was rocking him with her foot as she smiled at the screen on her phone. Noticing me looking, Jenna swung the phone round to face me. 'Say hi to Caitlin,' she instructed. 'Cait, this is Casey, who I was telling you about.' She then turned the phone back to herself, even as the girl was saying pleased to meet you, and continued straight on with her conversation.

'Come on, Seth,' I said, holding my arm out. 'Let's leave Mummy to talk for a bit. We'll go get a biscuit and some milk.'

Seth grinned, kicked his mum, ducked away from what could have been a slap around the head and ran after me, sticking two fingers up at his mother on the way out.

'That's naughty,' I scolded. 'I told you before we don't have that in this house, and you know that.'

'Mummy said it's fine,' Seth said. 'It just means fuck off, that's all, and if I'm mad, I can say what I want.'

Oh, can you? I thought darkly. 'Well, *I* said you can't. Now, what biscuits do you fancy?'

'Chocolate chip cookies!' he said, scrambling up onto a kitchen chair.

'Well, that's very specific,' I said, opening the cupboard. 'And as it happens, you're in luck. Tyler went and got those very ones only yesterday. They're his favourites.'

'I know,' Seth said. 'He already told me. But I was hungry. Very, very hungry,' he added.

I stopped rummaging and turned to look at him. 'What do you mean, you were hungry? When were you hungry? Seth, have you eaten the cookies?'

He burst out laughing and started to jump around on the chair. 'Ha ha – you're so stupid! You were looking for the cookies and I've eaten *all* of them!'

Ignoring him, I turned around and marched back into the conservatory. 'Jenna, could you hang up the phone, please? I need to talk to you.'

Jenna rolled her eyes before telling her friend, *sotto voce*, 'Fuck*sake*, I gotta go, babe, it's probably Seth kicking off again. I'll ring you back in a bit, yeah?' She then threw her phone across her bed and gave me her attention. 'What's he done now?'

I perched on the edge of the small wicker sofa. I had no choice; it was the only inch not already occupied with stuff. 'I know it's hard, love,' I said, 'but you can't keep giving in to Seth when he's demanding snacks all the time. This is why he refuses to eat his meals – because he's filling himself up with rubbish all day. He's already eaten a full pack of cookies this morning and he knows we wouldn't allow that.'

Jenna looked at me as if I was talking gobbledegook, then abruptly stood up and unhooked her handbag from the chair it was hanging on. Opening it, she pulled out a handful of coins. 'Sorry,' she said. 'How much? A pound? Two pounds? What do I owe you for the biscuits?' Her tone wasn't sharp – just completely matter of fact. 'That's not the point, and you know it,' I said, 'but how do you expect us to help with Seth's behaviour if I'm giving him one message and you're giving him an opposite one? It's not helping him at all, love.'

I was aware that throughout our exchange Seth had followed me and was now right behind me, watching and listening to everything. Which made me feel a little stupid. I should have had this conversation with her later, not in earshot, not while he was so interested in the outcome. I'd heard him screaming at his mum for biscuits more than once since she'd arrived, and although she usually started out by saying no, she always gave in eventually.

There was no satisfying him either – he had her measure. If Mike or I were around, she would go to the cupboard and get them herself, but if she got him two out, he wanted three, if she got him three, he asked for four. If Jenna thought we weren't in the vicinity, she would tell Seth to go get them himself, and with the keys to the kingdom, he didn't hold back.

Trying to think of a way to salvage the situation, and realising that Jenna seemed unwilling to continue with the conversation as she was now fiddling with her handbag zipper, presumably waiting for more admonishment from me, I decided to continue so that Seth could hear me.

'Anyway,' I said, 'neither of us want poor Seth to get poorly from too many cookies, do we? Or to need the dentist because of toothache, so we need to make sure it's only the grown-ups who can give out biscuits.' I walked closer to her then, hoping to catch her eye and get her on board. 'So, could you help me for five minutes, please, and we will get all the things in the treat cupboard moved to one that's higher up?'

Jenna frowned, but at least seemed to have cottoned on, finally. 'Okay,' she said, standing up and seeming to be getting into the swing of things. 'And then little shits who think they're clever can't get to them,' she added pointedly.

Not exactly what Seth needed to hear, but close enough, I thought, though as we went into the kitchen, I did whisper in her ear. 'Little *monkeys*, love, please? We need to help him to stop swearing.'

Not least, I thought, because he needed to be in nursery – something I was still waiting for an update on, despite Christine's earlier optimism. And there didn't seem much hope of making further progress on the swearing front anyway – not now Mum was here reinforcing it. At least not yet. True to form, the minute we started to remove biscuits, crisps and other snacks from the cupboard I had always kept them in, Seth started to rage. He ran across the kitchen and tried to kick the cupboard door shut, almost smashing it into his mum's fingers, and screaming and spitting as he did so.

'Fucking slags! Get off my stuff!' he yelled. 'Fat bitches! My biscuits! My cookies!'

My mood sank to my boots. Yet another explosive outburst. It seemed my hope that he'd change once reunited with his mother was as scientific a theory as the moon being made of cheese. I managed to fend him off as I grabbed the last couple of packs, but the noise and screams were just deafening. And in the middle of it all, Jenna dithered ineffectually, her 'behave yourself's drowned out by the volume of his voice.

'For fuck's sake!' she shouted eventually. 'There are no more fucking biscuits!' then, to me, 'God! He's just like his bloody father!'

That conversation would have to wait for another time obviously. His father who was in prison? His father who might even have been her personal drug dealer? I'd seen that so often down the years – and the future-destroying impact it had on children – that if it turned out to be the case here, I wouldn't, sadly, have batted an eyelid.

What *was* Jenna's story? How had she ended up where

she was now? There was so much that I didn't know, and surely ought to. No, I didn't have a *right* to know, because I wasn't fostering Jenna. But if I was to help her, I needed to understand at least something of her life.

'You know, Jenna, sometime soon you and I should –' I began, but was immediately drowned out.

'I *hate* you!' Seth yelled at her. 'You stink of poo and piss!'

'Right!' I said, standing up and brushing crumbs from my joggers. 'I've heard quite enough of this, young man.'

I had, too, and to hell with the rules. I reached out, grabbed Seth's hand and, though he tried his best to pull away, held on. 'Jenna, can you go and see to the baby, please?' I said. 'And perhaps tidy your room up a bit, and get the washing sorted out. Seth is going to have some time out in his room. Come on, young man, five minutes until you calm down.'

My taking control worked precisely as expected. 'Okay,' Jenna said, clearly happy I'd taken it. Happy to be let off the disciplining hook, which she seemed pathologically unable to deal with. Which was not how things were supposed to go at *all*. And as she walked away, I realised that in order to have any semblance of a peaceful life, I *would* have to do this. I *would* have to be the one to take control. At least until I found a way to get the girl to listen, watch and learn, and so step up a bit. And, distressingly, against all the evidence of the last three days, become the adult, and the mother, Seth needed her to be. Time was short here. We needed to step up a gear.

For the next five minutes however, I didn't feel much like an adult at all. In fact as I sat on the landing carpet, my hand gripped around the bedroom door handle so that it couldn't be pulled open, and a raging child on the other side of it, booting the hell out of said door so hard that it vibrated through my whole body, I was astonished to find myself crying. I cried quietly, so I must have had some sort of control; it was, I knew, a mixture of exhaustion, pure frustration and feeling sorry for myself. But I was determined to sit this five minutes out, even if they felt like an hour.

I'm so glad I didn't have my phone with me at that point, because if I had, I'm sure I would have reacted too quickly. I'm sure I would have phoned Christine, or Sam Burdett, or even Mike, and would have confessed that this was all too much. But I didn't have my phone, so instead I had to sit and allow my conflicted thoughts to fight it out, Casey style, in my head. Searching wildly for the positives, that's when it really hit me. I couldn't even take a walk down to the local shop to clear my thoughts and take a breather! Not without dressing both kids and getting Mum to get organised, and then dragging them all along with me. And how would that give me ten minutes' headspace? I couldn't nip across town to my parents' house, for them to give me the pep talk I sorely needed, because, well, how on earth could I take Seth around to theirs?

I had bloody signed up to this, and only now could I see that unless I started to change something, and fast,

I was going to become another victim of this family's chaotic life, and how was that possible? *Think, Casey, think*, I told myself, furious at the thought of my being trapped inside the claustrophobic bubble of this little family, and there being nothing I could do about it.

The kicks against my back started to get weaker and less frequent, and the screaming had now subsided, so I pulled myself up and took a deep breath before speaking through the door. 'Okay, sweetie,' I said, 'I'm coming in now, because it sounds like you're deciding to be sensible.'

I pushed the door gently and Seth turned his back and ran to jump on the bed, turning away, curling into a ball and hiding his face from me. I sat next to him and automatically reached out to stroke his now-sweaty head.

'It's okay, baby,' I said, 'you know, that was really good, the way you got yourself to calm down. Well done, sweetheart. I'm really proud of you.' I decided then, on instinct, to lay down alongside him and hug him close against me – try to swaddle him in security and warmth. 'It can't be nice for you to always feel so angry, I know that, baby. But it's okay. I just want to help you to be happier, okay?'

Seth turned to face me then, and hugged me right back, which almost set me off all over again. 'I'm sorry, Casey,' he whispered. 'I won't do it again.' His eyes bored into mine, glittering with tears. 'I want be a *good* boy.'

It was exactly the vitamin shot of hope that I needed. No throwing in the towel. Not today, at least.

Chapter 11

It's been a long time since I've sat in a school science lesson, obviously, but I do remember the odd little fact or two. It was school science that taught me how to work out if an egg is fresh by putting it in a glass of water (something to do with osmosis), and it was during a physics lesson, I think, when I first heard the fact that for every action there is an equal and opposite reaction. I think it was Newton's third law (he who had an apple fall on his head), and something to do with motion, but I think the main reason it stuck was because it was so often true. Every time something good happened, particularly when it came to fostering, there was always a little part of me braced for the inevitable moment when something bad would happen to balance it out.

So it was with Jenna. A few days into her arrival came extremely good news. A call from Christine to say that a primary school not too far away from us had agreed to take Seth; he could join their nursery class from the following Tuesday, on a five-session-a-week basis.

Naturally, to me, this felt like some kind of minor miracle. Though I was in a better place with Seth emotionally since his confession to me that what he really wanted to be was a good boy, the words hadn't exactly translated into actions. Not that I expected some radical shift – these things take time, and a lot of patient interventions – but there was no evidence that he'd even remembered that he'd said it, much less tried to rein his raging temper in.

And there was no getting away from it. Jenna and he ended up at odds over just about everything, often only seconds after he refused to do as asked, with them ending up more like squabbling siblings than mother and child. She just didn't seem to have any useful strategies at her disposal to deal with his frequent, and sometimes inexplicable, meltdowns. Distraction, cajoling, encouragement, motivation – none of those maternal skills seemed to be in her armoury.

Which wasn't exactly earth-shattering news either. This was a young, inexperienced and vulnerable mother – only fifteen when she'd given birth to him – and who had probably never had any of them taught to her. And, as mothers everywhere know, what you let pass at age two becomes all the harder to manage at age four, and so on and so forth right up to the day when you have an out-of-control teen on your hands.

So I didn't judge her. Particularly because what little I did know of her background suggested that she'd been struggling on her own. Why had her parents not supported her better? Why had she left home so young? These were questions I felt I badly needed answers to. But my one gentle probing about her relationship with her parents was so quickly rebuffed – 'I really, really, *really* don't want to talk about that, Casey' – that I knew patience was required; I'd have to choose my moment.

In the meantime, I knew I must concentrate on trust; in building it by using the lightest touch possible (her default mode, perhaps not unreasonably, was 'on the defensive'), and by gently invoking her determination to win her case (which was a given), and suggesting strategies that would help her to do so. So, again and again, every time Seth went into tornado mode, I would simply urge her to pause and think before reacting, to see if she could find less combative methods than she was obviously used to using with him, to keep him on side without a nuclear-grade fall-out.

'Every time you do that,' I'd pointed out to her, 'you are positively reinforcing the idea that life is generally nicer when he behaves.' Similarly, I trod carefully when it came to the regular business of, after losing her rag with him, her then caving in anyway. 'Because each time you do,' I had explained, again, very gently, 'you are reinforcing the idea that if he keeps on creating, eventually you will always cave in. What does that teach him?' I'd added, hoping for confirmation that she'd got it.

'I don't *know*,' she'd said, exasperated. 'Casey, you don't realise what a little shit he can be. What am I supposed to do, then? Thump him?'

'Noooo,' I said. '*Obviously* not. But you need to assert yourself. Put him in time out, like I've shown you. Demonstrate consequences to him. Let him know that if he misbehaves there will *always* be consequences. And then follow through with them. *Every* time.'

'Yeah, okay', she would say. 'I'll do that,' she'd promise. Till, all too soon, it would happen again. And I'd genuinely wonder if, without huge support, she would be able to put any of it consistently into place, once – *if* it happened – she was mothering them on her own. And perhaps that was it – perhaps that was why she was where she was. Because she'd never learned about consequences herself.

And she was right, of course, he could be a little sh**, as she put it. So much so that I was regularly finding myself wondering if there was more than just inadequate parenting at work. Were there other psychological factors in play?

So I felt for her. And also felt a rush of rare optimism about the prospect of Seth going back to nursery. I refused to dwell on his previous experience (or more accurately, the previous nursery's), and concentrated on the positive of this regular routine, which would, I was sure, help us all – not least because it would also expose him to the scrutiny of a teacher; someone outside of our bubble.

Once we got him there, at any rate, but first there was the hurdle of deciding what regime we were to go for. We were to take him on the following Tuesday morning, and leave him for the morning, after which, all being well, they'd have him for the duration of his time with me. It was just up to us to decide whether he did five mornings a week or, if we preferred, two and a half days.

Since the decision was mine, I opted immediately for five mornings, as it would give us a routine from Mondays to Fridays; we'd all get up, we'd all dress, we'd all walk down to the nursery, Jenna would have mornings free to concentrate on Tommy, and perhaps for us to build our own relationship, and would be in a good place for whatever the afternoons would bring, which I hoped would be quality time with her older son. In my eyes, even taking my own sanity out of the equation, this was a total no-brainer.

Jenna, however, felt differently.

'But that's mad,' she said, once I'd rung off from Christine and relayed the good news to her. 'The two and a half days thing is a much better option. That way, I at least get a couple of days to myself. Can you change it?'

'To yourself?' I'd asked mildly. 'Jen, there's still Tommy to look after.'

'But he doesn't *count*,' she'd argued, looking like a petulant fourteen-year-old. 'He just sleeps mostly, so at least then *I'd* be able to get some sleep.'

About which I did sympathise, because night feeds *were* exhausting. But this wasn't about her spending two days semi-comatose. It was about doing the best thing for Seth's emotional well-being and, hopefully, as a consequence, making everyone's lives a little easier. 'Jen, love, trust me,' I said, 'this is the best way to do things. You can grab forty winks when Tommy has his morning nap – and that's *every* day, remember – and it'll help get Seth into a routine for when he's ready to start school.'

'But it's up to me, isn't it?' she argued, clearly not seeing my reasoning.

'No, love, it's not. But –'

'Ok*ay*. Ok*ay*!' she huffed. 'Whatever. You're the boss. But, *God!* Like, from now on, I have to get up and get organised and get the kids organised and everything, like, *every single morning*?'

To which I'd obviously pointed out that there was such a thing as weekends. But decided to stop short of making references to puppies and Christmas – well, just.

We had a nursery place. That was what mattered.

But as night followed day, that equal and opposite reaction was never going to be far away. So it was that now, in near darkness, at silly o'clock on Sunday morning, I was sitting in the conservatory, Baby Tommy asleep beside me, wondering how the hell I was going to tackle the onerous daily task of writing up my log of the previous day's events.

I have always tried to be diligent with my paperwork (however tedious and time-consuming), making notes and records as soon after an incident as I can, so it's an accurate recollection of what has occurred and is there to reflect on later if I need to. It also important for covering my back. For example, if a foster child had committed a criminal offence and claimed to the police that he or she couldn't have done it, because they'd been with me at the time of the offence. At such moments, I could immediately bring up a record of everything that had happened that day, and since it was always dated, and always emailed to my supervisors and managers too, it was an important, incontrovertible and date-stamped record. I was meticulous about doing it, however seemingly humdrum and unremarkable, because my records had been needed on many occasions and, in more than one case, produced in court as evidence.

With a mother and baby placement, however, the records are quite different. Although technically, and certainly in a case like Jenna's, it is the child or children who are being fostered, rather than their mum, the reporting obviously has to be focussed on the mother, and instead of typing into a blank diary sheet as we would for any other foster child, there is a specific template we have to use.

The template covers absolutely everything a mother is expected to do in a day. Things like getting up at a certain time, washing/bathing, feeding the children, playing with them, cooking, cleaning, laundry, etc., plus managing behaviour and putting them to bed. Keeping a detailed and accurate record is, perhaps, even more important in these situations, since it will almost certainly be presented in court, if a solicitor requests it, and it can be used either as a defence for a mum to keep her kids, or can go against her if it highlights her failures as a mum.

One thing I had to decide in Jenna's case was how literal I was going to be. There was a section on the forms that had the ominous heading 'other', and it was here I could expand further on any day-to-day incidents that would give a fuller picture of life with her and the kids. The problem was that if I was really literal, then, at least in black and white, it would look like Jenna was a terrible mother. For example, were I to write 'Seth was screaming and refusing to get in the bath so Jenna yelled, "Get in now, you little shit, before I wring your neck!"', well, a judge might reasonably assume that was an example of threatening and abusive behaviour.

The thing was, though, I knew that this was just how Jenna spoke – not just to her kids, but to pretty much everyone. It was obviously everyday language to her, what she'd been used to all her life, and although it wasn't nice, I knew she had no intention of strangling her son. Of course I spoke to her all the time about her choice of words, and a lot of the time she would consciously try to say something less colourful. So, me being me, I neglected to report such things and could only trust my instinct that this was the right thing to do. After all, I told myself, it was the big things they were interested in, the things that might prove that her children were at significant risk. (Though I must add here that I am well aware how derogatory language can inflict emotional pain on a child just as much as physical violence can hurt their bodies, but I figured that I could help with that in my own way – and I would, without involving the authorities.)

Which was why, only just under two weeks into Jenna's time with us, I was having to calm down and do a little soul-searching with a strong cup of coffee before writing up the first part of the weekend sheet.

After the good news about the nursery (the logistics of which Jenna seemed to have finally accepted), I was almost pleased when that evening she'd told me that as it was her friend's eighteenth birthday on the Saturday, the next day, she had arranged to go for a night on the town. 'So, you and Mike are okay babysitting, aren't you?' she asked hopefully. 'Only I've got a taxi booked for eight. And the social did say I could have some free time, didn't they?'

To be honest, I felt a flush of relief. It was tiring to feel constantly on duty as resident judge, and, yes, I did feel it might do her good to have a few hours to herself. Plus, Seth would be in bed by then and I knew that, if he did wake, he'd be less likely to play up when it was just me and Mike around. (Which would definitely be the case, because Tyler was now spending every Saturday night with Naomi; out on the very outer reaches of my radar scope was the feeling that he had fallen for her hard and fast and deep. I could only hope the feeling was mutual.)

113

That being said, however, I still felt I needed to point out that there were ways and ways of going about things.

'Yes, they did, love,' I said, 'but they also said you had to give us notice, ask us if we felt like babysitting and be clear to us about exactly where you are going. Also, I believe that they don't expect you to be drinking alcohol during all this court business. You will keep that in mind, won't you?'

She'd rolled her eyes at that. 'God, it's not like I'm a raging alcoholic! I'll only be having a few drinks and, as for notice, I only found out myself yesterday!'

I took this one on the chin. It was important to choose my battles, but I still needed to be clear where she stood. 'We're fine to have the kids, Jen, but I will expect more notice if there's to be a next time, okay? And I will have to write it up, you realise that, right?'

'*Grass* me up, don't you mean?' she said, which struck me as unhelpful. 'Fine. Do what you have to. I'm not a prisoner anymore, Casey, and you guys are getting paid as the foster carers – you told me that *yourself*. I'm not being funny,' she added, presumably noticing my now less than sanguine impression, 'but I do all the hard work.' She sighed a heartfelt sigh. 'I really need a *break*.'

I think I might have notched up the 'angry foster carer' expression a little at that point, but just before I said anything I would have regretted, Seth charged into the living room and spat right into his mother's hair.

'I heard what you said, you slag!' he screamed. 'You're

not going clubbing with all those wankers, you're staying in your room!'

As had happened before, I was mesmerised by the way he articulated what he said – that it seemed so obviously something he'd heard someone else say. It was almost as if he was an angry man trapped in a tiny body. Or had spent way too much of his short life around angry men. Before I had the chance to say anything, though, Jenna grabbed him by the neck of his hoodie and pulled him roughly towards her.

'You dirty little bas ... boy!' she yelled, glancing at me and belatedly checking herself. '*I'm* the grown-up, and I do what I want. You're the kid, you do as I say and don't dare talk to me like that!'

'Gerroff me!' Seth growled as he bared his teeth and leaned right into Jenna's face. 'If you go out, I'm reporting you to the social and the police will come and send you back to jail where you belong, you nasty bitch!'

'Right!' I barked. 'Enough! Jenna, you go make up some bottles for Baby, and then give him a bath. I'll take Seth to help me make tea, and then you can give him his bath. I'm sick of hearing all this swearing and name-calling in my house. I will not have it!'

Both looked at me in surprise and then Seth ran off to the conservatory, shouting, 'My programme's on, don't wanna help no one!'

I left him to it, because for the moment it suited me. Instead I turned to raise my eyebrows at Jenna, waiting for her to do as I'd asked.

'Okay,' she said, more subdued now. 'I'm sorry. I'll go and sort Tommy out. But I was going to have a bath. And I need to wash my hair. I mean, I've got to get ready and stuff, haven't I?'

She added an apologetic half-smile, which nearly had me wavering. Nearly but not quite. 'Oh, were you now?' I said, at least allowing myself to return it. 'Well, unfortunately, as you've left it until now to tell me, I'm afraid there won't be an awful lot of time for that now. Love, you need to put the kids first. That's just how it is. If you were in your own home and had a night out planned, and had organised a babysitter, then that's what you'd be doing, wouldn't it? That's what you'd *have* to be doing. What you *will* have to be doing. Because that's how it works. So skedaddle,' I added, looking down to check my watch. 'If you look sharp, maybe you'll still have a bit of time for pampering.'

She didn't need any further encouragement.

And, to be fair, she did manage to pull it out of the bag, doing everything I'd asked of her (nothing like a bit of motivation) before settling the baby and quickly getting showered. Even Seth surprised me, making no fuss about his own speedy bath, and sitting nicely on his mum's bed, in his pyjamas, watching her putting the finishing touches to her hair and make-up. He even told her how beautiful she looked and how nice she smelled. 'Like a garden,' he told her.

So I was pleased with her. And also pleased that I could write that in my record. Mike was too – so much so that he even offered to drop her in town, so she didn't need to get a taxi and could save her precious cash. Which *was* precious – she'd need to save every penny she could. And despite my repeatedly reminding her that we had a budget for the things the children needed, she was constantly ordering bits for them from various websites.

'Seth's right,' I told her as she left, all dolled up. 'You smell lovely. What perfume is that?'

'Only a cheap one – I get them from one of those online discount sites.'

'Well, it doesn't smell cheap. It smells *gorgeous*,' I said, giving her a quick farewell hug. 'You have a brilliant evening, okay?'

I should have predicted it, of course. This was a nineteen-year-old – and one on a rare night out in town. And nights out in town, these days, rarely finished at eleven – as I knew from my own kids, at least half of the bars and clubs in town, eleven was when they got going. So when, after a perfectly pleasant evening with Mike in front of the telly, it got to eleven thirty, the time we'd agreed Jenna would be home by, I had that all-too-familiar sinking feeling. And when, almost as if pre-ordained, it inched round to midnight, it sunk even further. Mostly with the realisation that there were no two ways about it: tomorrow morning, I was going to have to write yet another damning note on her record.

Not home at the time agreed.

And perhaps worse? By now, of course, I was up and down like the proverbial yoyo, every time I heard the sound of a car out on the road. I'd also tried texting, then calling, but her phone was going straight to voicemail, so she either had no signal, was busy dancing or had turned off her phone.

Mike had gone to bed by now, to read – he'd played two hours of football that morning, so for 'to read', I read 'to fall immediately asleep' – so I was on my own down in the living room when my mobile trilled to life. It was an unknown number so as I swiped to answer it, I was already braced for it being a police officer.

It wasn't.

'Are you Casey?' a drunken female voice slurred. 'The foster carer?'

'Yes, this is me,' I answered. 'Who is that? Is Jenna with you?'

'Yesh,' came the answer.

'Then can you put her on the phone, please?'

'I'm sho shorry,' the girl said. 'But she can't come to the phone. She'sh a little bit worsh for the wear so she asked me to call. She got the train to mine with me so ima take her round her mum's house, okay?'

'But –'

'Is fine. Honest. Ish just round the corner. Ish *fine*. She said to tell you she'll text you the address in the morning. You can pick her up then, okay? G'night.'

'Wait!' I shouted. 'Is that Caitlin?'

But it was already too late. The girl had hung up and I had no number to redial. So that was that. There was very little I could do – nothing I could do – because I wasn't Jenna's foster carer. Had I been, of course, I could have called the Emergency Duty Team, but, as it was, I had no grounds for doing so. The only thing I could do, which I did, was send her a text, asking her to get in touch with me first thing so I could go and pick her up.

In the meantime there was the small problem of a tiny, weeks-old baby, who, though now asleep in the conservatory, a few metres from where I was sitting, would, during the night, need a feed, probably two. And since I couldn't exactly cart the crib upstairs and relocate him to our bedroom, meant a night – a broken night – in the conservatory for me too.

I was just preparing a couple of bottles (Jenna not having done so) when I heard the front door go. It was Tyler.

'Still up, Mum?' he said, grinning and making a show of checking his watch. 'Shouldn't you have turned into a pumpkin or something?'

He was merry. But only that. Drunk only on love. 'Don't even go there,' I growled, banging the lid down on the tin of formula, while he peered in the fridge for a bit, finally pulling out a carton of orange juice.

'Where's Jenna, then?' he asked.

'Don't even go there,' I said a second time. 'Passed out at her parents, after a heavy night, by all accounts.'

'*Ah*,' he said, pouring juice into a pint glass. 'Well, in that case I don't envy her when she has to face you tomorrow. Seriously, though, they're not going to let her keep those kids, are they? I mean, really? The way she carries on, it's like she's still a kid herself.'

Which were my feelings, too. At least in the 'kid' sense. But at the same time, she was making progress, wasn't she? And at least she'd been responsible enough to have her friend call me. That counted for something, at least in my eyes. As did what little I knew of her background. She was starting from such a low point, but that didn't mean she couldn't rise. 'I don't know, love,' I said, feeling the weight of it pressing down on me, and realising what a tonic it was to see my son looking so happy. 'Anyway, enough of that. How was your evening? Do anything nice?'

Tyler downed a good three of inches of juice before answering. 'Watched a bit of Netflix. You know, chilled.' Then he grimaced, and suddenly blushed right to his temples. 'Anyway, I need my bed,' he said.

'Ditto!' I answered, grinning wryly. 'But listen, love, you really must bring Naomi over. It would be so nice to get to know her better – especially seeing what a smile she's been putting on your face. Bring her round to tea one night, yeah? Dad and I are dying to meet her.'

He nodded, 'I will,' he said. 'Soon. I promise.'

'Do,' I told him firmly. 'I know we're a bit of a madhouse at the moment. But, lol, when are we ever not?' I added, grinning.

He placed a kiss on my cheek. 'True, dat,' he agreed. And it wasn't till he was halfway up the stairs that it hit me – I knew what 'Netflix and chill' meant, I was sure I did.

But nice though it was to know our son was having fun, as soon as I returned to the conservatory and my long baby-minding vigil, my anger returned. Because 'responsible' call or otherwise, Jenna had not returned home to us. To her *own children*.

So, given what I knew social services were thinking, what exactly could I write that wasn't going to significantly reduce Jenna's chances of keeping her children? And more to the point, would my conscience even let me?

Chapter 12

Mike appeared in the conservatory just as I was folding the sheet and fleece blankets I'd grabbed from the airing cupboard in the small hours, in the dark. Though a little chilly, it hadn't been too bad a night, as nights go, as the baby had only woken once, and settled quickly after I fed him, and the only other interruption had been my phone pinging at 3 a.m. A text from Jenna, with the address I should come and get her from, and *I'm so, so, so sorry. I've fucked up big time, haven't I?*, which, given the hour, I hadn't replied to.

And with morning, and an extra couple of hours sleep under my belt, had come a more pragmatic and positive mindset. Yes, she had, but, on the other hand, she *hadn't* been completely irresponsible. It felt as true this morning as it had last night – that her having had the where-withal to get her friend to call me, despite being inebriated, *had* shown that she was capable of being responsible. And her text in the night – whether still under the influence, or with the beginnings of a hang-over – had at least been an apology, which counted for something as well. So, though she was right that it wouldn't look good in my report, her subsequent actions would at least mitigate the damage. And, hand on heart, how many young parents, particularly as young as this one, hadn't messed up the way she had at least once?

So, on balance, though not good, this wasn't necessarily as bad as she probably feared. And you never knew, it might help concentrate her mind.

'She never came home then?' Mike asked, rubbing his eyes as he spoke. It was a little after seven, the sky just beginning to lighten, from impenetrable black to a deep, sooty grey. This was the worst time of year for a new baby placement, I reflected. Way too many hours of darkness to live through every morning, and way too little spirit-lifting daylight.

I told him what had happened, and showed him my phone. 'So I suppose I'll give it a couple of hours then go and fetch her. I doubt there's much point going now. She'll probably still be asleep.'

'And did *you* get any sleep, love?' he asked.

'Enough. More than I expected to, to be honest.' I looked across at the baby, who was deeply asleep himself now, black lashes (his hair was dark, as opposed to Seth's dirty blond) twin commas on his rose-tinted cheeks. Like every other baby ever born, he was perfect. To my eyes, at any rate, because every baby is. *What's life got in store for you, little man?* I wondered. Then it hit me again that there were things I had to write and, within that thought, came the next – that I personally had a lot of influence over that. Which wasn't a comfortable thought with which to start my Sunday. 'I need coffee,' I announced, bundling Mike back out through the doors into the living room. 'Let's have five minutes' peace before our pocket rocket's up, at least.' At which point, as if my words had been beamed directly to his brain, the rocket in question came thundering down the stairs.

Seth, as it turned out, didn't seem in the least fazed on discovering that his mother wasn't there. Which was perhaps nothing to be surprised about, since she'd only been back in his life for a short time and, in as much as he felt secure anywhere or with anyone, Mike and I had almost certainly begun to fulfil that role.

Which was not ideal, since I was already increasingly feeling that Jenna was finding that difficult – it was hard for her to assume control as a parent when Mike and I were so obviously the heads of the household. And a bit of a poser, too, given that the objective of her *being* in our household was to help facilitate the bonding of their little family unit so that, ideally, come the end of the assessment period, there would be minimal disruption when (or if) they moved back into their own home.

But this was far from an ideal situation, much less world, and just seeing Seth's indifference to his mother's absence made my mood begin to plummet – just how could I help steer her with her parenting of him without coming across as a kind of 'mother superior' myself?

I made a mental note to think about different ways of supporting her so that, as far as possible, I could step back and let that bonding, that last-word parenting, happen, however much of a mountain it seemed in practice. Because, though I modelled what I considered to be the best way to parent – and on an ongoing daily basis – I had serious doubts whether she was actually taking enough in, given the short amount of time she had to learn it.

In the event, rather ironically, we had a pretty peaceful breakfast. Bacon and egg baps, with lashings of ketchup, and Seth the best-behaved I had seen him in a while now, on account of a promise that if he was a good boy, he could spend an hour afterwards in Tyler's room, playing on the PlayStation with him – a treat of momentous proportions.

Which left me free to go and collect Jenna from her parents while Mike stayed home and took care of the baby. Except that by the time I'd texted Jenna and was ready for the off, Baby Tommy was screaming blue murder and would not be mollified, despite both of us working through the usual tick list of solutions. He was just a baby who was crying for no discernible reason, as babies so often do, and growing more pink and hysterical by the minute.

'Just go and fetch her, Case,' Mike told me. 'I've got this.' (He hadn't.) 'If he doesn't pipe down, I'll put him in the van and take him for a drive. Actually, there's an idea. Why don't *I* go and fetch her?'

I considered. I'd already worked out it would be an hour and a half's round trip, Jenna's parents living right out on the other side of town from us. Plus, I knew Mike needed to work on his van today; it had been playing up, and he'd planned to strip some component or other down before it packed up altogether. I was light on the details, car mechanics not being my area of expertise, but I did know it was likely to take a bit of time, which he wouldn't have if he went off to fetch Jenna. Plus, should he take Tommy out in it at all while it was playing up?

On the other hand, there was no way he could even start fixing while in charge of a baby. Seeing him struggling now (baby's cries are the very *worst*, aren't they?), I had a thought: 'How about I just take him with me?'

'You can't, love,' he said. 'Rules, remember?'

He was right. One of the rules being that if the grandparents wanted to see Seth and Tommy, they could only do so supervised, at a family contact centre. Right now, that was academic, since – another significant point – they hadn't even asked to. Not once. And I just had this strong instinct that *I* needed to go and fetch her. That if she needed persuading then I'd be best placed to do it. But the rules were still rules and I broke them at my peril.

Except I didn't even need to. Not strictly. 'I won't take him in. Jenna can come out to the car. And if they do want to see him, they can do it through the car window

– that won't be breaking any rules, will it? And since they've not shown any interest in doing so it's probably not even going to be an issue. Plus, needs must. Come on,' I said, holding my arms out, 'give him here.'

Needless to say, faced with my logic (plus a screaming baby), Mike didn't argue, and ten minutes later, I was on the road to the address I'd put in the sat nav and Tommy was once again fast asleep. And if it did turn out that the grandparents wanted to meet him, then I'd cross that bridge when I came to it, and the 'rules' bridge as well. I'd use my own judgement, write up everything in my notes and deal with those consequences, if it came to it, as well.

My forty-minute drive took me to a part of town I'd not visited in a long time, and an estate that my memory flagged up as familiar, from as far back as my pre-fostering days. I'd last been here back when I'd run the behaviour unit at the large local comp, visiting the home of a troubled teenager I'd never forget, Leo, who'd been caring for his disabled mother under the radar. It was sobering to realise just how long ago that was; by my reckoning, he'd by now be in his early thirties. I hope life had changed for him for the better.

The estate clearly hadn't. And as the sat nav announced that I'd reached my destination, and I began to feel anxious, it wasn't because of where I was. Far from it. I had been to many estates like this over the years, every house almost an exact replica of every other, gangs of youths hanging around on street corners – all staring at me with curious eyes as I searched for somewhere to park – unkempt little ones playing out in the rows of equally unkempt gardens and a cacophony of sounds – sounds that seemed normal in this type of environment, yet, if at some semi-rural development out on the fringes, would have people complaining to the council.

Not me. Even though I knew some of the local youths would be dealing drugs, I didn't feel alien here. Possibly because of my work (though, conversely, perhaps it was *why* I did my job), I felt a strong sense of kinship with the people who lived here. Because behind closed doors there were people of all ages and backgrounds, many of whom had faced really difficult challenges, who looked out for one another, who had a strong sense of community. Which wasn't sugar-coating it – there would also be all sorts of villains and petty criminals here – but the word 'neighbour', I knew, really counted for a lot here.

No, the reason I felt anxious was because, while I'd been making my way here, my mobile had been pinging like mad, with multiple text messages, and though I obviously hadn't been able to read them as I was driving, my phone was clipped to the dash in a holder, and I could see from the notification banners that it was Jenna.

As soon as I'd parked, a few doors up from the house number I'd been given, I took my phone from its holder and read them.

Mommy, Please Don't Leave

Jenna – Sorry, Casey, I was drunk last night so I came to Mum's cos I was ashamed of myself and anyway I probs wouldn't have woke to feed Tommy. I hope you're not mad.

Jenna – I'm guessing you are mad?

Jenna – I know I'm a shit mum. I'm sorry, ok? Been talking to Mum, she said I can stay here for a bit. And she's right. The kids are better off with you at the moment. I'll still fight the court case, but what's the point of staying at yours? I will only mess up again and it just makes it all worse. Don't come get me.

Jenna – Casey?

Jenna – You could at least fucking answer! Yes, I fucked up and I'm sorry. Tell the social whatever you want, they were always going after the kids anyways. Just please let Seth FaceTime each day cos he'll be upset.

I texted Jenna back. *Have been driving! Am outside. Three doors down. Please come back. I can't come in because Tommy's asleep in the back.* Then added '*Am NOT mad*', and pressed send. Then, when I knew it had been delivered and then, a second later, read, I sat and waited for her to emerge from the front door.

A minute passed. Two. No response and no emergence. And now I couldn't, of course, go up and knock on the door, because it would mean leaving the baby out of my sight. And no way would I do that – not here, not anywhere – which meant I'd have to unstrap the baby seat and take him with me. So I tried again: *Jenna, please just come out and come back with me.* Then, after reflecting, added, *This isn't the end of the world.* But, yet again, there was no response, either from my phone or from the house. Nothing for it, then, I decided, when ten minutes had passed. I'd have to take Tommy to the doorstep.

I grabbed my bag and climbed out, irritation beginning to rise now. I didn't know what was behind this – was it her or (how it had sounded) more her mother? – but what I did know was that if I didn't persuade her to come back with me, *now*, her case would take a dive that it would be hard to recover from. Not terminal, no, but definitely approaching it.

I unstrapped the seat (always a manoeuvre that seemed ridiculously more fiddly than it should be) and pulled it out of the car, Tommy now beginning to stir, looped the handle over my arm and headed back up the street. What were the parents' names? Janet and Phil? Or was it Janice? I wasn't sure I'd even seen their first names written down. The only name I knew for sure, because I had definitely seen it on the paperwork, was their surname, which was Buxton, same as Jenna's.

And as if Mrs Buxton had read my mind and my intentions, the front door flew open just as I turned up their path, revealing a short, plump and smiling grey-haired woman. After her smile, which looked slightly on the manic side, the first thing that struck me was her age. Either life and her genes had been particularly tough on her, or she'd been even later than I'd imagined having Jenna. I had no idea which, but she looked nearer sixty than forty, though she seemed as animated as an excitable teenager. I also realised that she must have been watching for my arrival, and seemed delighted – despite there having been, as far as I knew, zero contact – at the sight of her new grandson.

It was a lot of seemingly contradictory information to take in. And even more disarming was that, as I approached, she started yelling back into the house: 'Phil! Jenna! She's here! And so's the baby!'

'I'm Casey,' I began, unnerved by the volume of her voice. 'I've –' But she barely caught my eye, so eager was she to get a closer look at the baby. 'What a little beauty you are!' she cooed, poking a finger into his cheek. 'Let's go in and see your grandad, shall we, eh?'

With no sign of Jenna, I had just the two options. Either stay where I was, and ask her to ask Jenna to come and talk to me, or do as she seemed to think what I was going to, and follow her into the house.

I chose a middle way, not yet moving, but smiling politely. 'Janice, is it?' I asked her. 'Is Jenna okay?'

She glanced at the handle of the baby seat – was she hoping I'd hand him over? – then, for the first time, she seemed to take stock of me.

'Ha!' she said brightly, and it occurred to me – was she *drunk*? 'That one will *always* be okay,' she said sarcastically. 'If she fell into a bucket of shit, she'd come out smelling of roses. Come on,' she said, flapping her hand around in front of me, 'she's inside. Thinks she's staying here, but she's bloody well not! We've only just got over having Seth all that time.'

More information to process. And one question at least answered. It wasn't her mother who wanted her to stay, clearly. A picture of the state of play was building in my mind now, to go alongside the other one, the picture Christine had painted, which, as I followed the woman through the tiny hall into the living room, now exploded into glorious technicolour. It was exactly as she'd described, only more so. An almost-empty litre vodka bottle took centre stage on the coffee table, surrounded by beer cans and ashtrays full of butts. One armchair was completely filled with what looked like laundry – clean or dirty, I couldn't tell – and Jenna's father was slouched in an armchair in the corner, fag on the go, creating clouds of smoke, and grinning inanely.

My first thought, then, was for Tommy, and Seth, in absentia. On health grounds alone those children absolutely should not be here. The air pollution probably rivalled that of Delhi.

Jenna herself was on the sofa, sprawled out the entire length of it, and covered with a coat – not the teddy-bear coat she'd gone out in last night, but a big faux-fur leopard print number.

Janice (at least I thought so, she hadn't actually confirmed it) now marched straight up to her – lurching slightly, wide-legged, before correcting her trajectory – and roughly shook her shoulder. 'Wake up and face the music, pisshead,' she told her. 'No use hiding in shame, girl. The lady's here to take you back and, in case you're interested, your baby's here too.'

It was in such sharp contrast to her tone with me only a few seconds earlier that it blindsided me slightly – made me feel I was in the middle of a badly scripted sit-com. It also clarified what I'd thought about Seth's use of language. This was how they spoke to one another, clearly.

Jenna emerged, by slow increments, from her animal print shroud, to reveal that she also had the teddy-bear coat on. In fact, she looked as though she hadn't moved from the sofa all night – as if she'd staggered over there, flopped down and not moved an inch. She had one false eyelash fluttering, half-hanging on, half-hanging off, her phone clutched in her hand as if super-glued there, and, I could see, as she swung around to sit up, she was still wearing her boots.

'I need a piss,' was her only comment to her mother's admonishments. She then duly got up, staggered past her, into the kitchen/diner beyond, leaving me standing awkwardly in the middle of the room, swinging Tommy in his car seat.

I'm not often lost for words, but I was struggling to find some – what were the right words for such a situation anyway? Jenna's father, apparently a man of few words (and then some), seemed to be preoccupied with replacing a battery in the TV remote, and her mother seemed only to have eyes for Tommy once again, who she continued to fuss over, and prod and poke and cluck at, as if I was as inanimate as the baby seat itself – her comments 'what a little belter', 'who's a gorgeous boy?', and so on, seeming not to require answers from me.

Finally (after what seemed an age, though it was probably only moments), she addressed me. 'She's not staying here,' she said, alcohol fumes now *definitely* evident, 'don't worry. She's got to learn to stand on her own two feet. Anyway,' she added, cooing again at little Tommy, 'd'you want a cuppa or d'you have to get off?'

Despite the assault to all my senses I felt mightily relieved. Jenna might have given up on the placement, but I hadn't. Because there was no doubt in my mind that if she didn't come home with me and back to her children *now*, there was almost no way that the council would rescind their care order for them.

'I'm fine, thanks,' I began. 'We've really got to get back.'

At which point, Jenna, coat now trailing from her hand, reappeared. 'I've told you, Casey, there's no point going back now. They'll never let me keep them now. Didn't you read my texts?' Her eyes swam with tears.

'You bloody well aren't staying here!' her mother said. She jabbed a finger towards my face. 'You go back with her, you hear me? Sort yourself out, girl. I *told* you.

134

We've had enough of your shit. Tell her, Phil,' she added, nodding towards her husband, whose only comment on the matter was, 'Do as your mother says.'

'Or you go back into your own flat,' her mother went on. 'We've had enough of this.'

If I could have taken myself out of the middle of that room and looked down on it instead, I might have sat down and wept for her at that point. No time for that now, however, as I could see Jenna crumpling. Better to simply step in. 'You need to come home with me, Jen,' I said, touching her arm. 'The kids need you, and this would look really bad to the judge, you *know* it would. Besides, Seth starts his new nursery the day after tomorrow, and he'd be so upset if you're not there to take him.'

'But I'm not even *allowed* to,' Jenna pointed out plaintively. 'I just have to tag along while *you* do, that's the truth of it. They don't even trust me to take my own son five minutes down the road! What'd they think I'm gonna do – kidnap him or something?'

Quite the opposite, I thought, but obviously didn't say. The *truth* of it was that their principal worry would be whether she'd even manage to get any of them out of bed. Herself included. But her mother had other ideas.

'No!' she jumped in. 'What they *think* is that you're going to piss off again with that useless piece of shit, that fucking scumbag *Jake*!'

What? My mind immediately searched through its internal filing cabinet. Jake ... Jake ... Was that the name of Seth's father?

'You just had to, didn't you?' Jenna yelled at her. 'You just couldn't wait to bring him up, could you? He's just texted me. That's *all*! Why make my life even worse than it is?'

'Don't tell me you didn't meet up with him last night, girl,' her mother said. 'That frigging Caitlin is one of his best mates, you silly cow – I'm not *stupid*. You think I was born yesterday?'

'Look,' I said, switching Tommy's seat, which was growing heavy now, over onto my other arm, 'what's done is done, and we can work around it. But, Jenna, I didn't get any of your messages till I pulled up outside, love, or I would have texted you straight back this morning. There's no need for any of this now. Just come home with me to the children, and I promise I will have a word with social services about building up some trust, so they will allow you to take Seth to school on your own. I agree – it doesn't seem right me breathing down your neck with such a simple thing. And of *course* you wouldn't kidnap him. And if anyone suggests that that might be a risk, then we can counter that by you leaving Tommy home with me while you take him. How about that? That might work. What do you think?'

She sighed heavily. I could tell she was badly hungover. Dehydrated, too. I could tell by her taut and sallow skin. I needed to get her out of there. And Tommy.

And, as if to remind me, her father, who had seemed barely a part of proceedings, rummaged down the side of his armchair, the remote now abandoned, found what he was looking for, and lit another cigarette.

'Look, love,' I went on, while Jenna, sniffing, peeled off the last of the flapping false eyelash. 'You're not in any trouble right now, I promise. You are right, you're an adult, and you're allowed your free time. And you took the decision to stay out last night so that you didn't disturb us or the kids. Which is *fine*. And if you come home now, we can have a chat about all of this and start afresh. You deserve that, and so does Seth. He's only just got his mum back, after all. So, let's just go back and try to get him excited about his new nursery, eh?'

As I waited for Jenna to process what I'd said, I stored away the new information about Jake. That was another conversation, for another time and place. Right now, I had to make the girl see that if she gave up now she was playing into her doubter's hands. Which was the absolute last thing she must do.

I don't know if my thoughts reached across the room, as well as my words, but once again, after blowing out a long plume of smoke, Jenna's father addressed her.

'Get your coat and stuff, and go, Jenna,' he said coldly. 'It's only a matter of time before you fuck it up anyway, because you always do, but you're not living here while you do it. Me and your mum've got enough on our plates without all your shit.'

I clamped my mouth – which was now beginning to open – firmly shut, and instead gave grateful thanks for all the good people in the world. Of which I knew there were far more of than the type sitting in the corner. I didn't know the history, how far towards the end of the tether she might have brought this man, or this couple, but what I did know was that there should be a special place reserved in hell for a father who spoke to his child in that way, whatever the circumstances, whatever the provocation.

I watched Jenna's chin jut. 'Don't worry,' she said, addressing him directly. 'I'm out of here. I don't want to *fuck up* your invalidity benefit claims, do I?' She threw her coat over her arm and picked her handbag up from where it lay on the floor by the sofa. She then grabbed the handle of Tommy's car seat and took it from me. I didn't argue. 'Say bye to the grandson you are *never going to see again*. Oh, and by the way, Seth's right. You *stink*, Dad. Come on, Casey, let's go.'

Her mother, glassy-eyed and swaying, flopped down into the nearest armchair, sending another gust of fetid breath my way as she burped. And that was apparently that. Neither parent made any move to stop their daughter, to say anything, or to even glance at the baby. Just sat there, in their two greasy armchairs, in total silence. I coughed nervously and followed Jenna to the door.

'Nice to meet you both,' I said, feeling stupid. 'Thanks for keeping her safe.'

Her father snorted and rolled his eyes at that. 'You'll learn, lady,' he said, almost under his breath. 'You'll learn.'

Chapter 13

As soon as we were in the car, Jenna started rootling in her bag, eventually pulling out a pair of oversized sunglasses, which she clamped on her face before resting her head against the window and groaning. They seemed an unlikely thing to carry about on such a dark February day, but, given that she was one of the Instagram generation, I didn't pass comment – I reasoned they were probably integral props for various selfies.

Their deployment was also indicative of her hangover kicking in, and – more to the point – that she probably wasn't up for any weighty discussions. Something confirmed when I gently enquired if she was okay, to get the three-word response, 'No. I'm dying.'

Which was a shame, in-car conversations being one of my tried-and-tested strategies for discussing things kids couldn't quite say face to face. But there was nothing to be done about it but make the journey home in silence, my only company, since Tommy had fallen straight back to sleep, the soft tones of my golden oldies radio station.

Which wasn't on loud enough to drown out my thoughts, specifically about what her father had said to me. 'You'll learn,' he'd said. Well, he was right about that. Mine was the kind of job that involved a lot of learning, and the last half an hour had gifted me plenty to study, including the comment about 'Jake', and the questions that sprung from it, something I'd run by Christine as soon as I had the opportunity. Not that Jenna didn't have a right to text – or see – anyone she chose to, apparently out-of-jail ex-partners included. And it wasn't appropriate to make a call on the relative merits, or otherwise, of such a situation. He had presumably done his time, and might have turned over the proverbial new leaf. Who knew, after all? Perhaps he wanted to play a part in Seth's future.

And what about Tommy? Who we already knew was effectively fatherless? Something that, tragic though it was, didn't exactly surprise me. Not given that heavy substance abuse was involved.

I supposed only time would tell. But, in the meantime, the most enlightening aspect of this morning's adventure had been that unedifying glimpse into Jenna's upbringing. That had been sobering in itself. Was it any wonder she was where she was, given the circumstances? I didn't know how long her parents had been living the way they did, and knew nothing about their disabilities either. What were they? Since her father hadn't moved from his armchair, perhaps he couldn't walk? And I'd definitely spotted a couple of inches of heavily swollen, mottled skin between his trouser and his sock. Though there was no evidence that I could recall that he had walking aids. And if they were both on disability, which was what I'd been told, what did they consist of in Jenna's mum's case? At some appropriate point, if I could, I'd ask Jenna.

Though, in reality, did it make an iota of difference? They clearly had no time for her, for all her mother's drunken fussing over Tommy, and I doubted they'd be any support to her going forwards – no, if she got to keep her kids, she'd be on her own.

My thoughts turned to Seth. He'd lived a month with those two people. In that environment. In that squalor. Which I'd known about, obviously, but now I'd seen it for myself, it really brought me up short. No wonder he had the behavioural issues he did. Incredible that he didn't have even more.

We returned home to find that the boy in question had, for the most part, behaved well, only kicking off once, over the number of biscuits he'd been allowed (a shitty two?) when Mike let him have a snack just after I'd left.

And despite his indifference earlier, he seemed genuinely pleased to see Jenna, running straight up to her, throwing his arms around her legs, and starting to tell her all about the game he'd been playing with Tyler.

To my huge dismay, though, she pushed him away.

'I'm not well, babes,' she told him, and, with the sunglasses still in place, looking for all the world like a trumped-up reality show diva. 'Mummy's hungover, yeah? I need my bed, so just leave me to sleep for a bit, yeah?'

Still holding the baby, as I was, I was quick off the blocks. Quicker even than Seth.

'Um, I don't think so, Jenna,' I said. 'I have work to do, then I also have a roast dinner to prepare. And don't look to Mike and Tyler,' I added, as I saw her gaze snaking past me. 'They've done more than their fair share of childcare already. I'm afraid you're going to have to entertain your children, love, hungover or not. Take some painkillers, drink a pint of water and splash your face. As mums, we make choices, good or bad, just like kids do, and, again, just like kids do, we have to deal with the consequences.'

I was writing up my report in my head as I was speaking. *Jenna understood the consequences and, despite being hungover, she rose to the challenge ...*

Though not without first making it known that I was the witch bitch from hell, taking Tommy from his baby seat and dragging herself off into the conservatory without speaking a single word of thanks to me, Seth following forlornly in her wake.

I watched him go, thinking how much nicer it would have been if he could instead go out into the garage and potter in there with Mike, but I couldn't have that, no matter how natural it felt. As one of the children we were fostering, those were the sort of things Seth would have otherwise thrived on; being part of a normal family, doing normal family stuff, however seemingly everyday and mundane. But I couldn't allow it. These were Jenna's children and this was one of those days when the hard lessons about the realities of being a parent were really learned. And it felt doubly important, given what I'd seen of her own parents this morning. This girl would have no one to support her. And even if they'd wanted to, they would not be considered fit to. Which made the tragedy of it all feel even more acute.

Sadly, once I sat down to update my report, I knew I must not give my emotions free rein. So I kept it concise, reflection-free and to the point. I reported that I'd agreed to have the children while Jenna went out with a friend, but that I had assumed she would be home that night. I then ran through the sequence of events from when she'd asked her friend to ring me right through to her anxieties about whether it was worth continuing with the placement, because she'd already decided there was little or no hope and that I'd managed to convince her that it was. I also noted, in summary, the environment I'd found at her parents' and what they had said about her not being welcome there anyway.

What I *did* leave out was her inability to function properly due to her hangover, because I struggled with my feelings about that. I imagined that a lot of mums have had a bit of blow-out once in a while and felt just as rough as Jenna the next day. And just as they had to, I'd made sure she had done exactly that, even if it did mean that the whole little family had had a very lazy day, mostly spent curled up on Jenna's bed, watching movies. She'd learn.

Mike had been in and out of the kitchen, where I was working on my laptop, throughout. 'You really going to let her get away with this?' he asked as he came in to grab his umpteenth wodge of kitchen roll. 'Only I remember the odd times when Riley would wake up in a mess after a night partying with friends, and there's no way you would have stood for her spending the whole day in bed. You losing your touch, Case?'

'No, I am not!' I said, jabbing him in the backside with my ballpoint. 'And get out of here with your oily hands – look, you've got it all over the cupboard handles now! If you must know, I'm taking a different approach, that's all. Playing a longer game. Jenna is a completely different kid to our Riley. If I were to carry on with her today, nothing would sink in. All she would take from it is that I'm just like every other adult in her life. Someone to be afraid of, someone she can't trust.'

'So, she gets a free pass then?' Mike asked, stepping away from the point. 'Sulks and locks herself away and then avoids any discussion or explanation?'

'Not at all,' I said. 'Now go and finish whatever you're doing on the van, love, and trust me. As far as Jenna goes, tomorrow is another day.'

In the meantime, the rest of that day was particularly peaceful. And I realised that there was a model for doing this kind of placement that could make life a bit easier all round – at least on my own stress levels. I could simply step back a bit, and treat Jenna and her children a little more like lodgers, after all. They had their own space, and I'd provided all the basics, so it wouldn't be a huge leap to let them function more independently, and for me to let Jenna manage Seth more on her own. After all, my most important job was to help her live independently, in readiness for the day when the children were formally removed from our care, and Jenna would be allowed (and I refused to accept this wasn't still a possibility) to have them back and do exactly that.

But that wasn't me at all. As dogged as it sounds, in order for me to help both Jenna and little Seth, I had to purposely push buttons, expose their triggers and then deal with the aftermath in a way that might, hopefully, leave an impression, and add to her so far meagre stock of parenting strategies. It was hard, and would mean continuing to operate at extremely high stress levels, but in order to understand the chaos of their lives (not to mention the mystery of Jenna's past life), I had to be right in there with them, in every moment. Because it was there, in the eye of the storm, that I could see more clearly, not least in terms of Seth's behaviour, which was still as puzzling as it was challenging, something that became apparent a day and a half later – on Tuesday, his first morning at nursery.

Monday, as it turned out, had been cheeringly positive. With nursery in the offing, I'd decided to take our little troop to the big supermarket out on the edge of town, so we could buy Seth a few bits and bobs – a little backpack, some new trainers, as he was almost out of his current ones – and a couple of new outfits to wear. I also wanted to get a couple of things for Baby Tommy too. Like any other baby, he was fast growing, and growing out of his baby grows and, though I had a huge stash – all sizes, all ages – I had an allowance for such things and intended to spend it, as both babies and four-year-olds went through clothing like biscuits and, as things were right now, the washing machine was on twice a day.

Jenna, who I kept forgetting was unaware how fostering worked, seemed embarrassed and a little guilty that it should be this way. It was also a question of pride, I realised, about providing for her little ones, which I felt was very much to her credit.

'I've got money,' she assured me, as we wandered along the clothing aisles.

Which was true, she was currently on Universal Credit, but I also knew that as I was obviously fostering Seth and Tommy, she'd be on the single-person payment, which was probably only £80 a week. And if she got the boys back, she'd need every penny she could get.

'It's fine,' I insisted. 'While the children are being fostered the council are responsible for feeding them and clothing them, so please don't stress, love. Keep your money – try and save up, if you can. Build a rainy-day fund up. I've got this.'

'But I need to contribute,' she'd argued, showing

a maturity that impressed me. 'I *want* to contribute. I *should*.'

She'd then surprised me, having accepted that I was paying the supermarket bill, by dashing back in, while I was putting the shopping in the boot.

'I need some tampons,' she'd said. 'You okay for a minute?' But had then re-emerged, not with tampons, but with some daffodils and tulips. For me. 'They weren't expensive,' she promised as she thrust the bunches at me. 'So, I wasn't being extravagant. I just wanted to get you *something*.'

It had been all I could do not to burst into tears.

But ying being ying and yang being yang, Tuesday morning began as Monday's polar opposite.

It began, true to form, with the usual meltdown. Which started up just as I was waving Mike off to work.

'What the hell is going on in there?' he asked, wincing at the racket coming from the conservatory. 'God, the neighbours are going to *love* us,' he added, hurrying out of the door.

He was right. It was twenty to eight, the dawn only just broken. And the neighbours to our left had only recently retired, and were enjoying – so they'd told me only a month or so ago (ouch) – not having to get up and commute any more.

'You fucking *are* going to school, you little shit!' Jenna was shouting. 'And I'm going to tell 'em what a bad boy you are when we get there!'

'Fuck off, slag!' Seth screamed back at her. 'I'll tell the teacher all about *you*, you bitch, I'll run away! I'll fucking kick you till you bleed, an' I'll spit at all the kids!'

Tommy's cries entered the mix then, and hostilities abated, while Jenna was presumably changing his nappy or feeding him, and/or Seth had been distracted with the TV or something. Or biscuits. The rate they'd been disappearing lately, I didn't doubt she had a supply squirrelled away.

I waved Mike off and, hearing the sound of Tyler in the shower, went into the kitchen to lay out some breakfast. Perhaps I should think about laying the table the night before, I decided. With four adults needing to get up, washed and dressed now, getting organised was going to be a military operation, with Jenna and I getting ready, of necessity, in shifts. At least today we had the luxury of an extra bit of time (the school had suggested we arrive fifteen minutes after everyone else so that the teacher, Mrs Sykes, could help Seth to settle in), but from tomorrow we would need to up our game. But could Jenna rise to the challenge? I knew she'd struggled to get Seth to nursery when it was still just the two of them. But rise to it she must, because if things went her way, she'd have to do this, along with Tommy, on her own, every day – and hopefully without all the shouting and swearing.

Table laid, and a row of bread slices ready in the toaster, I went and put my head round the conservatory door, only to find Seth licking out the inside of a chocolate wrapper (was *that* why he'd stopped kicking off?), the baby on the floor without his nappy on, looking chilly, and Jenna sitting on the bed, straightening her hair.

'*What?*' she said, when I pointedly looked at my watch. 'There's loads of time before we have to leave. *Chill.*'

'We have to be there –' I checked my watch again – 'in less than an hour. Which isn't a lot of time to get everyone washed and dressed and ready. Plus, we both still need to shower.'

She waved the hair straighteners at me. 'Nah, you're alright,' she said. 'You go ahead.'

'Aren't you going to?' I asked.

'Durr, *no*,' she responded. 'I might shower later. I showered last night already. And Seth doesn't need washing. He's fine as he is.'

Judging by the state of his face, that was questionable. 'But he does need to dress. And he does need some breakfast,' I pointed out.

'Don't want none,' he said.

'He's alright,' Jenna added. 'You go and have your shower. We're cool.'

At which point, a depressing vision of their future 'school mornings' pin-sharp in my mind's eye, I did as instructed and went up to get myself ready. As with every aspect of parenting once one child becomes two, she would, of necessity, learn.

In the meantime, it was me who got the pram out, me who wrestled Tommy into his snuggler, me who found and insisted upon hat and gloves for Seth, me who did his coat up and me who found a spare pair of mittens for Jenna – it being me, and only me, who had thought to check the weather, and establish that it was only five degrees above freezing.

It was around a fifteen-minute walk to the local primary school and nursery, and I was keen that we walk rather than me drive them down there as I felt the fresh air and exercise would be good for all concerned, and not least because when the time came for Jenna to have the boys back, she would not have the luxury of a door-to-door chauffeur, and managing her time to factor this in would be essential, even if the nursery Seth ended up at, assuming Jenna got them back, was only a short walk down the road from her. Which, in reality, it probably wouldn't be.

And perhaps because he was nervous, or just because he wanted to wind up his mother, Seth complained bitterly the whole way.

'I'll run away, I swear to God I will,' he grumbled, almost to himself. 'I hate school. I hate teachers. I hate stupid nursery. Nosey bastards like the social, they are.'

'Where on *earth* does he get all this stuff from?' I asked Jenna, as he stomped long ahead of us. 'He can't possibly just think those sorts of things up himself.'

Jenna shrugged, shrinking her head even further into the collar of her coat. 'Where do you think?' she replied. Which kind of answered my question.

'Well, I hope he tones it down when we get there,' I

said. 'I'd be mortified if he came out with any of that in nursery.'

But it seemed Seth had other ideas. Or at least had decided that since he was being made to go anyway, he might as well make it easier on himself. Because as soon as we arrived at the gates, a total transformation happened – his whole body language seemed to change before my eyes. I don't know what prompted it – perhaps the sight of the school buildings in front of him? – but as soon as he saw them, it was as if the Seth we knew had been spirited away by aliens, and a completely different child substituted in his place. His stomp slowed to a saunter, his shoulders relaxed and a genuine-looking smile slowly spread across his face.

I'd seen this with him before, of course, but it was still something to witness. Had he made a decision to be the good boy he'd talked about?

'Good morning!' he called out to a passing adult. 'I'm the new boy!'

I glanced at Jenna, assuming she'd be as encouraged by this as I was, but was irritated to see that she was otherwise engaged. Still holding the pram, yes, but with her head bent towards her phone, as she was busy sending a one-handed text. Seth saw it too, and for a moment I saw his expression change. But then he smiled even more widely and held out a hand for me to hold.

He went up on tiptoes and cupped his hand around his mouth. 'Casey,' he whispered, 'can I tell everyone you're my mum?'

I could have wept, as well as cursed, but I wasn't sure Jenna had even heard. 'Oh, sweetie, that's nice,' I said, 'but seeing as you already have a mummy, how about you just tell them I'm Aunty Casey?'

'Aunty Casey,' he said, nodding. 'Oh, okay.'

'Anyway,' I hurried on, 'shall we take you to meet your teacher? The entrance to the nursery is just over there, see? By the windows with all the different coloured balloons painted on them.' Then, pausing only to dig Jenna in the ribs with my elbow, I led our little party across the playground.

The teacher I'd been told to meet, Mrs Sykes, was already standing in the doorway – at least I assumed it must be her because she waved as we approached. She was in her forties, I judged, and looked warm but also matronly – as in I imagined being matron to a crowd of teenage boys wouldn't faze her any more than the tots in her charge.

'Mrs Watson?' she asked me when we reached her. I smiled and nodded. 'And you must be Seth,' she added, squatting down to say hello to him. 'Welcome, welcome. Would you like to come in and say hello to everyone? We've all been dying to meet you.'

I felt Seth's grip tighten round my hand, but the smile remained fixed. 'You're coming in with me, aren't you?' he whispered, as Mrs Sykes stood up again.

'Yes, of course,' I reassured him. '*And* Mum, of course,' I added. 'This is Jenna,' I added to Mrs Sykes, 'Seth's mum.'

152

She'd hung back a little and I realised she was *still* bloody texting! But all eyes on her now, she stuffed her phone into the pocket of her coat. She was nervous, I realised, her cheeks now staining with a blush. She seemed to struggle, too, to meet the teacher's eye.

'Well, it's lovely to meet you too, Jenna,' Mrs Sykes added warmly. 'Come on in out of the cold a minute, while we show Seth where his peg is. And I'd *love* to take a peek at his little brother. Can I?'

So in we trooped, Mrs Sykes helping Jenna to get the pram over the door sill, and Seth immediately tugging at my hand. 'Wow,' he said in wonderment, 'it smells like Christmas in here!' causing me to wonder just how much time he had *actually* spent in his previous nursery. It was as if we'd brought him into a magical cave of wonders, and I felt sad to think he'd almost certainly only be here for a short while. I knew Jenna's flat was too far away for him to come here, and if she didn't get them back (though I didn't want to dwell on that option), he might even end up being fostered out of the area.

Still, he was here now, and good things could come out of this new routine; it would add some structure, social skills and education.

The baby inspected in short order, by both Mrs Sykes and a young woman called Chloe, who was apparently her teaching assistant, Mrs Sykes turned her attention back to Seth. 'So, young man,' she said, 'shall we take a quick tour of the classroom while everyone else, as you can see, is sitting nicely on the mat? Then we'll do all the introductions. That sound okay?'

I smiled to myself at that 'as you can see'. I had a happy hunch that Mrs Sykes was the sort of nursery teacher who'd deal with poor mat-sitting etiquette in short order.

Seth nodded. 'Can Aunty Casey come too?'

'How about Mummy?' I suggested. 'I imagine she'd love to have a look around, don't you?'

Seth shrugged. 'If she wants.' And I felt my heart sink again, not least because as Mrs Sykes led our little group all around her classroom, the multiple pairs of eyes that were following our progress seemed to make Jenna shrink even further inside her coat. *Ask something*, I thought. *Show some interest. Engage.* But while I oohed and aahed and pointed out all the fun things to her excited son, she shuffled round as if the proverbial cat had got her tongue. And when Mrs Sykes asked her if she'd started any reading with Seth, she mumbled something about not being near a library and turned beetroot.

'What was all that about?' I asked her when, Seth having been left – and apparently happy for us to go – we headed back out through the gate into the street again.

'What?' she asked.

'You, love. I do wish you'd taken a little more interest. Are you okay?' I added, turning to look at her properly. 'You looked very ill at ease back there. Were you? I know it can be a little intimidating, going into a new school, meeting new people, but –'

She glared at me. 'Wouldn't *you*?'

I was shocked by her vehemence. 'I don't get what you mean, love.'

'Wouldn't *you* be embarrassed walking into that place, knowing they *all know* you've just come out of prison? That you're a complete fuck-up. That you're not even allowed to look after your own kids and have to trail around behind their foster mother like you're a child too?'

Caught on the hop, I didn't know how to answer. Because, of course, she was right. Mrs Sykes almost certainly did know. That particular fact, along with the reason they were living with me currently, would have been front and centre in the school's discussions with Christine. Would have been the reason, more to the point, that they'd given Seth that much sought-after place.

Her eyes had filled with tears now, as well. So, as she was pushing the pram, I rummaged in my bag for a tissue, though she was already furiously wiping them away with a gloved hand.

I gathered my thoughts. 'Yes, love, they do know.' I outlined the reasons why. 'But you must stop thinking you're an EFF-up, because you're not. Not at all. You've just been through an extremely hard time. But you've come through it. That's what matters. And you *are* look-ing after your own kids. At least you were last time

I looked. And sweetheart,' I added, as she stopped to blow her nose, 'please don't for a minute think anyone in that school is judging you, because they're not. They want the same thing as I do. As we *all* do. For this all to work out for you. We all –'

'But they *do*. Everyone does. I'm not stupid. I know *exactly* what people think of me.'

Exactly what your horrible parents have drummed into you that they *think of you*, I thought, but couldn't quite bring myself to say. At least not yet. These were her mum and dad – the only ones she had. Though, judging from my own impressions of them, perhaps that day would – and should – come, however painful it might be for her. 'Well, you're wrong,' I said instead. 'And if people do judge you, well, the best defence against *that* is to simply prove them wrong.' I started walking again, before we all froze to the spot. 'Jenna, you *can* do this. Look at you – you're young, fit and healthy. If you want to keep your children then you *can* keep your children. You've just got to believe in yourself a bit more, then roll your sleeves up and get on with it – it's not rocket science, honestly! – so the courts see the evidence that you can. It's just a question of *doing* it, putting the hours in, putting them first, and –'

'But how *can* I?' she said. 'Even my own *son* doesn't want anyone to know I'm his mother!'

I could have wept as well then. So she *had* heard.

Chapter 14

As every parent learns once their first child goes to nursery, those few precious hours of freedom fly by astonishingly fast, as if calibrated using a completely different system.

No sooner had we defrosted and had a coffee, and Jenna had attended to Tommy's needs, than it felt as if we were preparing to set off to pick Seth up again. To be fair, today's session had been shorter than it would normally, but, even so, it was a valuable lesson for Jenna in how managing your time when you had free (well, freer) time to manage gave you more of it. Which was a precious, not to mention sanity-saving, thing for any parent, but particularly so for someone like Jenna, who was likely to be parenting on her own.

I'd continued my little pep talk all the rest of the way home, mostly along lines that seemed important to discuss – the fact that what children said and what they felt were often very different things, and that she must try to see the things Seth said to her as not being from his heart, but more a reaction to the insecurity he'd suffered in life thus far, and, in their own way, a reflection of how much he *did* need her.

'When a child says "I hate you",' I explained, 'they almost never really mean that. They might mean "I hate that you've stopped me from doing what I wanted to", or "I hate that I've been found out in doing something wrong". Even when it's serious – say, a child who's been let down, perhaps by a parent who was supposed to come and visit them and didn't – I've seen that *far* too many times – that word "hate" doesn't mean hate, it's an expression of love. If the child didn't love that person so much, they wouldn't feel so distressed, would they?'

I stuck my neck out then, telling Jenna that I thought that, in Seth's case, it was mostly an expression of his understandable insecurity, having been separated from his mum for that period of time, and that he was probably anxious that he might lose her again, which, given the circumstances, was a hard thing to say.

'Of course,' I added, keen to lighten the conversation up a little, 'sometimes he says he hates you because he's *way* too used to getting his own way, and he knows *exactly* how to push all your buttons. And the best way to deal with *that* is to be firm and consistent. If you say no, you must *mean* no, every single time. If you do that, he will begin to learn where he stands – where he's safe and secure and the world feels less scary. And it's that, above everything, except your unconditional love, that will make him feel he's more on solid ground.'

Her answer to which was to burst into tears again. Hot, noisy tears and a heart-breaking admission: 'I've never felt on solid ground in my whole entire life.'

It sometimes felt as if tears were the currency of my job, because this admission, at my kitchen table, felt like payday.

By the time we arrived back at school I had started to convince myself that my main task over the remaining weeks of the placement was, more than anything, to try and build Jenna's confidence in her ability to be a capable enough mother to her children. It was easy to forget that she'd been a fifteen-year-old mum, and judging by what I'd witnessed at her parents' house over the weekend, one with precious little in the way of advice and support.

I also made a mental note to ask Jenna if she knew anything about the circumstances of her own birth. She'd come into their lives very late. So why was that? There were all sorts of possible scenarios up for offer. Was it simply that they had got together relatively late in life? Had they lost a child earlier and had their lives fallen apart as a consequence? Was this a second marriage? Had there been other kids, from previous marriages or relationships? Had they been known to social services at some other, earlier point, and perhaps had children taken away? And just what *were* their disabilities? (Well, beyond the bloomin' obvious.) And had they been a factor for all of Jenna's life?

What I really wanted to do was get her to properly open up to me, and perhaps this morning's moment was progress in that respect. But right now most important was that we get a routine going, and that, as a result, we could start to do something constructive about her fractious relationship with Seth.

I wanted that so much that I even crossed my fingers as we approached the playground – that he'd enjoyed himself, that he'd behaved himself and that he'd emerge from his session in the same sunny frame of mine as when he'd gone in.

Yeah, Casey, right. Because real life is *always* like that.

He'd barely been waved off by Mrs Sykes, with a 'see you tomorrow!' than he had Jenna in his sights, and not in a good way, his happy mask falling from his face like a stone.

I could see why, as well. We'd had a delivery during the morning of something Jenna had ordered online. My first assumption, opening the door, had been that she'd been buying herself some clothes. Like the little ones, she had precious few of them. But I'd been wrong. Because, in fact, using some of what scant money she had, she'd bought a little baby carrier – entirely on her own initiative – so she could strap Tommy to her chest when she was doing chores, or playing with Seth, and it would also mean she didn't have to take the pram out all the time. 'I read on the internet,' she told me, 'that if you carry your baby in a sling lots, it helps you bond with them better.'

This, in itself, obviously moved me, as did her comment that she hadn't told me about it because she knew I'd have insisted on paying for it if she had, or might have said it was too expensive for the 'social's allowance'.

So she'd taken the initiative and just gone ahead and done it anyway.

Naturally, she was keen to road test it on the journey back up to school, and I was so pleased at the development – something so clearly positive and uplifting that I could write in my report at last! – that it was gutting to see his response to it.

'What's *that* thing?' he demanded, as we walked up to meet him. Then he flung himself, bodily, against Jenna's legs. 'Pick me *up!*' he demanded. 'I'm *tired!*'

To her credit, Jenna immediately crouched down and put her arms around him. Which touched me likewise – she'd obviously taken in some of the things I'd said to her earlier.

But Seth was having none of it, wriggling free of her embrace. 'Put him *down!*' he demanded a second time. 'Pick *me* up!' Then he turned to me, his little face full of fury. '*Make* her. *You* have him!' he commanded me, before wilting theatrically, letting his knees and arms sag, as if he'd just emerged from a twelve-hour shift down a mine.

Which for him, I rationalised, might have been what it felt like, especially if he'd managed to keep control of his impulses for all that time. And now he was letting go, big time. But there was no way we were going to attempt the complicated business of unstrapping the fiddly carrier straps and doing a switcheroo between us out in the cold, and, as if realising, Seth kicked Jenna in the ankle.

'Ow!' she yelped. 'God! You little shit! That bloody *hurt*!'

'Good!' Seth spat at her. Then, his tiredness apparently forgotten, he set off up the pavement at a run.

Glancing round briefly, and pleased to see Mrs Sykes had gone inside now, I told Jenna 'I've got this' and hurried after him.

'Hey,' I said, catching up with him, and grabbing his wrist. 'Whoah, there. That wasn't a very nice thing to do, was it?'

'*She's* not very nice,' he huffed.

'And who is "she"? The cat's mother? And how can Mummy pick you up when she's got your brother strapped to her?' I let go his wrist, and held a hand out in its place.

He took it – an apparently automatic action. I squeezed it. 'You sure do like giving your mum a hard time, don't you? And you know what? A little bird told me that when *you* were tiny, she carried you round in a sling, just like Tommy's. That's what you do with babies –' I lifted both my arms, bringing his hand along with me. 'So you have both arms free for cuddling their big brothers.'

'Didn't *want* a cuddle. I wanted a *carry*. She shoulda brought the pram.'

Yes, I mused. *He's probably right. She should.*

But I certainly wasn't going to chastise her for it because I should have thought of that myself. I glanced back. Jenna was still a few steps behind, texting. Always *texting*!

I faced forward again, determined not to let things start unravelling, even if it was Jenna, and not me, who should be having this conversation with Seth. 'Mum was just giving it a try-out,' I improvised, briskly. 'You have to check these things work, in case you have to send them back again. Anyway, *more* to the point, how did your morning go, sweetheart? Did you have fun? I want to hear *everything* about it. What did you do? Did you make some new friends?'

'I played polices with Oscar,' he said. 'And I threw him in jail!' But he was smiling as he said this so I figured no one got chastised or hurt.

'Jail?' I said. 'Oh, my! Were you PJ Masks and was he a master criminal?'

He shook his head. 'No, a burglar. Burglar Bill. We were just doing polices. And I painted a picture but it's not dry enough to bring home yet. And tomorrow I'm sitting next to Sophia. She's a girl,' he added helpfully. 'And she's got yellow hair. What's for food? Can I have sausages and chips for my dinner?'

And there, it was done. That simple exchange was a building block that would, on some level, inform Seth that relationships with adults could be okay. That it was safe to be himself, that someone was interested in his day.

I turned back to Jenna, who'd caught us up now, and whose phone, I was glad to see, was back in her pocket. 'Did you hear that?' I asked her. 'Chips and sausages for dinner. And Seth's done a picture, haven't you?'

'What of?' she asked, reaching down to stroke his head.

He shook her hand off, clearly not ready to forgive her for the sling yet.

'Of you,' he said. 'You. Sent to *jail*.'

'Right, I think we need to institute a school-day routine,' I told Jenna as she made up a fresh bottle for Tommy, and I cut potatoes up for chips. Not my usual lunchtime fodder – I was more of a sandwich or soup type in the middle of the day – but today, what Seth had asked for, Seth was going to get; I wanted to rid this day of negative memories like sling-gate. Instead I wanted it to be the first of many positive ones in his immediate future. Well, as positive as could be organised, given the complicated dynamics. And having a structure would be a good place to begin.

Much better, certainly, than what was happening right now – that Seth had simply plonked himself down in front of the TV in the conservatory, and where, if I didn't take any decisive action, all three of them would no doubt spend the rest of the afternoon. And every afternoon after that, left to their own devices – literally:

one glued to the telly, one glued to her phone. Jenna's had been pinging non-stop since we got back.

'So I was thinking,' I continued, 'that once he's home every day and we've all had our lunch, we should ring-fence half an hour to an hour, say – whether Tommy's asleep or not, because I'll mind him for you – for you and Seth to have some one-to-one "together-time". You know, just to play together, uninterrupted, you giving him your undivided attention, so he knows he matters to you every bit as much as Tommy does. Which I *know* is true, obviously,' I added immediately. 'But will help cement that truth in Seth's mind. Plus, I think it'll do you *both* good,' I went on, 'and it's the sort of thing the judge will be pleased to see as well, because you making time for play, that kind of regular emotional enrichment generally, is one of those things that they really like to see. In terms of what you do together, it doesn't need to be anything elaborate,' I reassured her, seeing as her expression was now reminiscent of a child at a total loss about some tricky piece of homework being explained to them. 'Just, oh, I don't know – perhaps doing something crafty at the table. I have a craft box, all sorts of bits and bobs, so there's plenty to choose from, or, if it's dry, maybe a game of running around the garden, or perhaps a treasure hunt –'

'Treasure hunt?' Jenna looked as if I was speaking to her in tongues.

'Yes, or races – you could do a little mini-Olympics with him, or just play pretend, imaginative play – I have a *huge* dressing-up box, and he's just the right age. Though it doesn't even have to be structured; you can let him take the lead. It doesn't matter *what* you do, love,' I finished, 'just that you do *something* together. Something positive and happy, something that makes you genuinely feel enriched in each other's company.'

Oh, if only we could achieve that kind of nirvana, I mused. And as I did so, another notification pinged on Jenna's phone. If only *all* of us could, I thought, glaring at the thing. And might better be achieved if phones were banned from playgrounds, I decided. And parents – well, some parents – actually got involved a bit in play-time, and stayed in the moment, instead of looking upon it as a chance to take themselves off to social media and immerse themselves in other moments altogether.

I followed Jenna's gaze, which responded to the noise like a dog being whistled. I went back to cutting chips, determined to put my play-plan into action. Because, frankly, not all 'progress' *was* progress.

The trouble was greater than I could lay at the feet of mobile phones, though. The fact was that Jenna didn't seem to know how to play; it was all too evident as I watched them from the kitchen window after lunch. She'd managed the first bit – suggesting to Seth that they go and play out in the garden. And he'd responded immediately, suggesting they play 'polices' like they'd done at nursery, and even explaining in detail how 'polices' was going to work.

And he impressed me. Despite apparently having had so little play in his young life, he'd clearly been enthused by his morning at nursery, because he immediately took the lead; him being the policeman and Jenna being the 'bad man', instructing her to hide while he turned around and closed his eyes, then catching her and leading her to the designated jail – the space in the corner of the patio between two garden chairs. He'd found a little stick, too – his truncheon – for giving her a 'good kicking' (hmm, I thought, but it was what it was) when she tried to escape.

But Jenna looked a little like a fish out of water. Whether self-conscious or disengaged (perhaps a bit of both) she looked less like his mum than some distant spinster aunty, one who'd been drafted in to keep him occupied and hadn't the first clue how to do it. One who was hoping to pass the baton on as soon as possible – evident itself from the way she kept glancing at the kitchen window, as if hoping for permission to come back in.

It was sad. So, so sad. But also eye-opening. A window on a world I knew so little about. Both her former world with Seth, almost certainly dominated by her drug use, and the world she'd grown up in herself. Had she ever been played with as a child? I didn't think so. Not based on the evidence before me.

Still, somehow, they managed to eke out half an hour, and when they did come back in, Seth was pleasingly flushed, both from the cold, but also from the exertion.

As was Jenna, who it occurred to me was spending unhealthy amounts of time indoors, and probably not getting enough daylight and vitamin D – the health benefits, especially in the winter months, were undeniable – yes, physically, but also mentally, too.

I was just about to say so when the doorbell went. Another parcel delivery. Which I went to retrieve, while Jenna and Seth took off their coats.

It was addressed to Jenna again, so I took it back into the conservatory to give to her. But she shook her head on inspecting it, and smiled. 'You open it.'

I had Tommy in my arms, so I passed him over to her. 'But it's addressed to you,' I pointed out, as we swapped package and baby.

'I know,' she said. 'But it's for you. It's a present.'

I opened the jiffy bag to find a box inside, and a dispatch note, which she took from me. Inside the box was a bottle of perfume. 'Impression', it was called. Not a name I immediately recognised.

'It's a knock-off,' she clarified. 'Well, not a "knock-off". Not as in dodgy. It's the one I had on at the weekend,' she explained. 'They're dead cheap, but they smell soooo like the real ones. Amazing, isn't it? I thought, since you liked it, I'd get you some too.'

'Oh, Jen,' I began. But I couldn't manage much more. I was too busy doing an impression of someone crying.

Chapter 15

Call me Pollyanna, but the events of Tuesday had really lifted my mood. After the negatives of the weekend, it was so nice to be able to sit down with my laptop and write so many good things in my daily report. Needless to say, then, that I went into that Wednesday – Seth's second at nursery – feeling really upbeat and positive. And, perhaps equally needless to say, the positivity rug was soon pulled out from under me, along with my imagined routine.

Because, of course, I *had* imagined it – to go something like this. We'd all be up and ready to leave the house every morning at 8.45 a.m. We'd either drive round to the school or have a brisk, bracing walk, chatting about the day as we went. On arrival, Seth would run happily into his classroom and then Jenna and I would have a precious couple of hours that we could spend playing with Baby Tommy, and talking (oh yes, we would) about her past, and how best we could start shaping a brighter future for them all.

The reality was that mornings were horrendous. By Friday, day four, Seth had declared he hated school, and by the following Monday, he declared war on mornings altogether. So the following week we had a new routine in place – one quite different from the one I'd envisaged. He'd scream the house down no matter who tried to dress him; would head-butt and spit, curse at everyone, and kick, even though he knew it was a battle he couldn't win. Then, on the way, he would run off without warning, and pick up stones to throw at passing cars or people. To top it off, either myself or Jenna (the sling, at least for school-run purposes, now abandoned) had to physically pick him up and carry him the rest of the way, kicking and screaming. Once there, as per the routine Mrs Sykes had put in place, we would leave immediately, right after handing him over.

I've never been one to underestimate the amazingness of teachers, obviously, but Mrs Sykes and her TAs were on a whole other level, dealing with Seth and his sometimes near-hysterical meltdowns with the sort of calmness and composure you'd more normally associate with people running a bring and buy sale at an old people's home.

The calmness and composure were not without foundation. Because every day, at pick-up, just before handing him over, Mrs Sykes would reassure Jenna (*always* Jenna, not me, bless her) that the very minute we were out of sight, Seth would quickly compose himself, join his friends in the nursery and then behave mostly impeccably. 'Though he does display some idiosyncratic behaviours,' she added to me at one point. 'So we're keeping a close eye on him. Might be worth further investigation.'

Which pleased me no end. Perhaps Seth's behaviours weren't just down to his upbringing to date. And if that were so, it might mean precious access to additional support. And in the meantime the hours between 9 a.m. and 11.45 a.m. were such a relief. It meant that, however bad things had been, I always had this light at the end of every day's tunnel; a period when I knew I could take a breath, take stock and get myself battle-ready for the next steps.

It also gave Jenna precious respite from the never-relaxing business of mothering two small children, one so often determined to try and thwart and/or undermine her. One thing I hadn't managed, however, by the end of the next week, was to have any really meaningful chats with Jenna about her background, and what had shaped what had happened to her.

Not that I hadn't kept trying; something I was even keener to do since having had that glimpse into her former world. More than once I'd tried to open discussions; about what her own experiences of nursery had been like, about school and friends generally, but it was weird – almost as if she had PTSD about it – how quickly she would move to shut me down, either by immediately changing the subject or, on one occasion, by baldly stating that she didn't want to, and wouldn't, 'discuss my parents', leaving me feeling chastised for interfering in her business.

I had to remember, of course, that she'd never been in care, or even had any prior dealings with social services. So she'd never been through any psychological assessments (well, as far as I knew), or been through the kind of counselling process that's common with children in care. And it was only my business in so far as it might help me guide her better through *this* process, so if she didn't want to talk about her past, I couldn't make her. I could only hope the time would come when she did. Because I really, *really* wanted to find out about her parents – even if only to confirm my worst fears.

What I was able to do, however, was have multiple chats with the various professionals involved in Jenna's care and case. Now Seth was in nursery, they had all evidently decided to make hay while the sun was shining, even if it wasn't, which for the most part it wasn't.

This also seemed to be the case for Jenna. Towards the end of that week, for the second time in as many days, she got a call from her solicitor, who wanted to go through some things in preparation for her first, mid-placement, court hearing.

She'd gone into the conservatory to take the call, but since I was in the living room at the time, dusting, and her voice was so raised, it was impossible not to hear what she was saying. 'What you on about?' she was saying shrilly. 'Listen, mate, I don't know where you've got your info from, but it's wrong!'

She listened for a few moments, then put her hand over her speaker. She clearly *wanted* me to know what was going on anyway. 'He's a dickhead!' she mouthed at me, before continuing. 'I don't *think* so.' Then, 'Well, it doesn't *sound* like you're on my side. You're meant to be arguing *for* me, not *at* me. And you'd best tell them that my mum's a fucking *liar*, mate. She'll do anything to see me on my arse – *none* of it's true. I don't even know where Jake *is* these days, let alone have anything to do with him!'

Jake again. My heart sank. So what had been said? What had happened? I was just wondering what kind of fresh complication this would be when my own mobile chirruped into life: it was Christine.

'Just checking in, Casey,' she said, 'I was off the back end of last week – Dad-in-Law problems, I'll fill you in later – but I just had a read-through your recent reports and emails and thought I best give you a quick ring. How's nursery going? Everything settled down again after the incident?'

I went into the kitchen and closed the door behind me, leaving Jenna still ranting to her solicitor.

'Well, as settled as this family can be,' I told Christine. 'Nursery is going well – they have Jekyll, we have Hyde – but I'm glad you called, because it seems there is some "Jake" complication, and I could really use some intel on the current situation. He was mentioned by Jenna's mother the weekend before last, as you know, and I'm worried that he might be on the scene?'

But it seemed she wasn't phoning me to talk about Jake. She had another remit altogether. 'I'm not up to speed on that,' she said. 'Not yet, anyway. Listen, I was calling about Jenna's sleepover at her parents. Just to, well, keep you abreast about things there.'

I was confused. The event in question was almost two weeks old now. What things did she mean? Then the penny dropped.

'Just so you know,' she went on, and in a tone that was familiar, 'the managers had a bit of a meeting while I was off. Discussing the incident. And while there's nothing to stop Jenna doing what she did, it was kind of frowned upon, as you probably anticipated. But, erm, well … as was the fact that you took the baby along with you when you went to pick her up.'

'With good reason,' I explained. 'Which I pointed out in my report. And –'

'Absolutely,' she interrupted. 'Which I *totally* take on board. It's just that they're saying – and Casey, I can't argue this – that you put the baby at risk, and that, actually, the way the family are, it's not beyond the realms of possibility that they could have taken the baby from you and thrown you out of the house. And before you laugh,' she hurried on, 'of *course* I know you wouldn't have let that happen, but I also know you understand that such a thing would be deeply traumatic for a baby, even one as young as he is.'

Laughing I most definitely was not. I took some deep breaths as I let Christine's words sink in. As if Jenna's father – apparently disabled as he was, would ever have managed, or even stirred sufficiently to even think about doing such a thing. As if her drunken mother would either, despite all her cooing. The pair of them couldn't have been clearer that they couldn't wait to be rid of her. Of us. Of Tommy as well. And (a key point, I thought) they had called social services precisely because they wanted rid of Seth, hadn't they? I related all of this, with feeling, back to Christine.

'Yes, I see where you are coming from re Seth. Of course I do. But their point is that you couldn't have known how they would react to seeing the baby. Not beforehand. And it could equally have been that Jenna had gone there with different motivations. Perhaps they'd had a change of heart, for example, and suggested she go back to live with them. Which I'm not saying was likely –'

'Too right. They hadn't even asked for a contact visit, remember?'

'Yes, I *know*, but the fact remains that you took him inside the house, into an unknown situation, where he might have been at risk ...'

She left it hanging, and me with my inevitable thoughts. In fact, I had decided when I'd written it up that I wasn't going to try and argue my case, should I be asked to, beyond pointing out the choices I was faced with that morning, and accepting that the one I made wasn't ideal.

So I didn't. 'I can only apologise, Christine,' I said, knowing she would have to go back to management with whatever I said, and that there was little point in causing further conflict. 'It wasn't an easy choice to make at the time, as you can imagine. On reflection, I really should have anticipated there being a situation where I'd have to take Tommy into the house with me. I should have stayed at home with the kids and got Mike to go and collect Jenna, and if it happened again, that's what I'd do. It's just that on that day,' I added, not being able to resist pointing it out, 'I did believe Jenna would be more likely to be persuaded to come back if I went to get her.'

'I know that, Casey,' Christine said gently. 'Of course I do. And I didn't phone to criticise your judgement. But they expect you to know that it's *only* the kids we are concerned about here. Jenna's choices are hers to make, and if she messes up, then …'

'Then she loses her children,' I said flatly. 'Yes, I get it.'

'Casey, you are doing an absolutely brilliant job,' Christine said, her tone changing again, to one Mrs Sykes might have used on Seth. 'And management think so too. One hundred per cent. They acknowledge that few would have even agreed to a placement like this, much less stuck it out the way you have. Please don't let this upset you. You know how these things work. We have to be seen to be ticking the boxes, because you know as well as I do that we're damned if we do and damned if we don't.' She sighed. And then paused, as if choosing her words. Which it turned out she was. 'Can I be frank?' she said finally. 'You need to harden your heart. Just a little. I know you well enough to see how this happened – it's because of who you are – someone who was never going to find it easy not to think of Jenna – and that's to your credit. But be careful. It's just not worth having the powers that be on your back, love.'

I paused too, feeling guilty. Feeling sorry for Christine. I'd put her on the spot, having to relay all this, and I knew she would have fought my corner tooth and nail before phoning me. She had my back, always. I must not forget that. She was only the messenger here.

'I know, and you're right,' I said. 'And you're right that I do care as much about Jenna as I do her children. I really want to be able to help her. In fact, it's impossible to have such a situation, and to leave her out of the care-giving. I just can't do that. To me they're a package, and the judge and children's social worker can surely see that, but yes, I will be more careful in the future about the judgements I make.'

Christine left me with a few platitudes, which (although I appreciated the vote of confidence) did nothing to lift my deflated mood, so when my mobile rang again, almost immediately after, I wasn't really in the right frame of mind to take another round from Sam Burdett.

'I've just explained everything to Christine, Sam,' I said, assuming he was ringing to cover the same ground. 'I can send you a more detailed email if you need anything else?'

'No, no, I'm not calling about that,' Sam said, a hint of urgency in his voice. 'It's something else that's been flagged, and it's not good. Not for Jenna, anyway.'

Once again, I got that familiar sinking feeling as I listened to Sam explain that certain information had been passed his way: that Jenna *had* apparently re-established contact with Seth's biological father, Jake. 'Which, as you can imagine,' he finished, 'is a definite recipe for disaster. So we are putting another report in to the judge,' he went on. 'And we'll be saying that this relationship is a real risk to the children, so we won't be supporting any applications for Jenna to keep them. Not given what we now know.'

I was shocked by his bluntness. 'Is this hearsay?' I asked. 'Or do you have proof? Because other than when she went out for the evening the Saturday before last she hasn't been out of our sight since she arrived. I obviously don't have the facts, but even if she did have contact with him that night, does that constitute a relationship? And by you not supporting any applications in Jenna's favour, does that mean she will definitely lose her children?'

'Well, not definitely,' Sam admitted. 'But that's what we're asking for. She clearly can't be trusted.'

I don't know if it was just because I'd had my knuckles rapped, but I felt immediately angry. He barely knew the girl, let alone whether she could be trusted. And more than that, I was beginning to think he barely knew the role of a social worker either. He had the sensitivity and diplomatic skills of a tent peg. I was that furious. Even more so by what he said next.

'And yes. Relationship. We've been told they conduct it over the phone for now, but a source who overheard a conversation between them has informed us that they are planning to meet up again, just as soon as the opportunity presents itself. So what we're asking you to do, Casey, given what we know, is to try to be privy to any conversations Jenna has on her phone, and if you overhear anything untoward, write it up and send it straight to me, please.'

Who the hell *was* this guy? Sherlock bloody Holmes or something? And who did he think *I* was? James Bond?

'Are you being serious?' I asked. 'You're asking me to eavesdrop on her conversations? I'm sorry, Sam, but I don't think I can do that. And quite aside from how distasteful that is to me – which it is – Jenna usually conducts her private calls to friends at night, after the kids are in bed, and often after we've gone to bed too.'

I was stretching the truth there a little. Well, a lot. Jenna did chat most of the day on the phone, and as she tended to call everyone 'babe' or 'sweets', and ended almost every call with 'love ya', I had no idea if the person at the other end was even male or female. And more to the point, she was never furtive about it. If she was secretly phoning her ex then I felt fairly certain that the middle of the night would be exactly when she did it.

Which she might well be, because – I groaned inwardly – all those texts.

'Well, do your best,' Sam said, apparently impervious to my words, much less my tone. 'And in the meantime, could you please make sure you expand your diary sheets a bit more? They all seem to be about Seth and what an efficient mother Jenna is. It would be helpful to have a little more about her day-to-day interactions with the children – her language, physical admonishments, confrontations, things like that.'

He sounded suspiciously like he was reading from notes – notes that had been highlighted as those most likely to throw light on Jenna's maternal deficiencies. Once again I got a clear sense that there was an agenda in play. That my instinct was right; they had already made their minds up about Jenna, and were expecting me to provide evidence to support that. So after making it clear that I had never seen her raise her hand to Seth, *ever*, I ended the call as quickly as I could, because I didn't trust myself to speak to him civilly. Who the *hell* did he think he was? The placement, as it unravelled before me, *was* all about Seth. There was no getting away from it. And if Jenna was to keep her children she would definitely need some professional help with him, because, without help, some of his ingrained negative behaviours would only become and more embedded. I was trying to make all of that clear in my reports, wasn't I? Wasn't that what I was supposed to be doing? And as for the bit about being an efficient mother, well, if the heading was 'Did Mum get up with the children?', I would of course answer 'yes'. If it asked 'Did she feed the children?', then 'yes' again.

They set the questions, I answered them. Yet there was obviously this subtext that I was supposed to get on board with. Had this been the unspoken assumption all along? That my *real* role was to provide evidence to prove their point? But wasn't I supposed to be impartial?

'You wanna know what that bitch has gone and done?' Jenna asked as she burst into the kitchen, waving her phone about. 'She bloody shopped me!' She stabbed the phone with her finger now. 'That was my solicitor. And he's useless! He only thinks my mum, my *mother*, the world's biggest *cow*, is a reliable witness for the social!'

Deep breath, Casey, I thought. Time to think and regroup. 'Calm down, love,' I said, putting down my own phone and pulling a chair out for her. 'Tell me what's going on while I make us a cuppa. I think we could both use a strong coffee, don't you?'

'I need a strong fucking *vodka*!' Jenna said, her chin wobbling and tears springing to her eyes. 'I just can't believe it, Casey. Except I can, and that makes it even worse!'

And now, of course, Sam's chippy phone call made sense, even if Jenna's solicitor worked in mysterious ways. He'd apparently asked her to level with him over any contact with her ex, coaxing her into doing so by reassuring her that it was in her interests to be candid and honest about everything, and that he was one hundred per cent on her side.

'But then I admitted it, and he went absolutely mental at me!' she railed. 'Called me a "silly, silly girl" – the complete *tosser* that he is – and said I was cutting my own throat. And then he dropped it on me that it was *my own mother* who had opened her gob! Been in touch with the social and grassed me up for turning up at hers drunk, and said she knew for a fact I was getting back with Jake. Apparently he's this "massive risk" and "basically a good for nothing". I mean, and they don't even *know* him! I *told* my solicitor that he's changed his life. I *told* him that he isn't like that anymore, but oh no, nothing I say counts for anything, because I'm rubbish – according to *them*, he's only out of jail on licence and it's just a matter of time before he ends up back inside again. I hate them all, Casey. *Hate* them. They've *all* got it in for me.'

Because I was busying myself with the coffee, I had my back turned, and I was extremely glad of it. It gave me space to assimilate this new torrent of information, and also to think, and I needed to because I had to be careful what I said here. Right now, Jenna believed that the whole world was against her, and, if my conversation with Sam Burdett was anything to go by, she might well be right. So she had to believe I was in her corner, even if the reality wasn't quite that black and white, because she needed to be heard without judgement or fear. And I very much wanted to listen.

I turned around. 'And *are* you getting back together with Jake?' I asked as the kettle started boiling. 'Is that what you plan to do?'

She exhaled heavily. 'I don't know, I really don't. And that's the honest truth. It's just complicated, is all. I mean, he's the only guy I've ever loved, Casey, so it's not like I can just switch off my heart, is it? And he's Seth's *dad*. And the only one who's ever loved us. Loved *me*.' She threw her phone down on the table, and sat down heavily. 'And before you say it, yes I *know* he was bad for me. I *do* know that now, whatever they've told you.'

'No one's told me anything,' I replied.

'*Really*?' she said. She looked surprised at this. Perhaps understandably, since her whole life was the subject of such scrutiny.

'Well, they said it was a "toxic relationship".' She made quote marks with her fingers. 'Like I'm an idiot. Like I didn't know about that kind of stuff. But I do know. I always knew. I'm not stupid.'

'They?'

'The counsellor woman. In prison. And everyone else besides,' she added with a wry half-smile. 'And the domestic violence people and the drugs counsellors, so I do know all that shit.'

I smiled back at her. 'Sounds like you do,' I agreed. 'Yet knowing all of that, you're still considering going back there? Back to that "toxic relationship"? Is that *really* what you want?'

She sighed again. 'No. *No*. God, though ... I don't *know*. I'm such a mess, Casey. I always have been. And he's been the only person ever who could see through all that. He understood me. Yes, he was handy with his fists now and again. But only when I pressed his buttons, you know? Stupidly wound him up.'

So, despite her 'knowing all that shit', she really didn't. She knew all the buzzwords, all the things the professionals wanted to hear, and to impart to her, but understanding the real truth of the relationship she described – that bit was obviously beyond her. She'd got no more than she thought she deserved, and she'd clung to it. Because she thought he 'understood' her. Understood what kind of girl would feel his 'handy knuckles' and not call the police, more like.

It was heartbreaking. As was the fact that in the space of an hour, I'd found out more about Jenna than I had in a month. Had found out *the most important thing*. That she had been playing with fire in a way that left everything to do with parenting her little ones in the shadows.

The question of Jake's merits, or otherwise, were for another day. What I needed to impress upon this girl, if she was to have any chance, was that *all* bets re him were now off. 'Look,' I said, 'chatting on the phone to someone isn't necessarily going to have a huge impact in court. Ditto texting. It's what happens *now* that counts. What you do to assure the judge that you can make safe choices. And I think you know what I'm going to say about what those safe choices are. I'm talking about stopping this relationship before it starts up again. You simply aren't in a position to argue his case. Not if you want the courts to let you have the children back. He may well be a changed individual – I can't comment, I don't know him. But I do know about the care system, and "may well be a changed individual" won't be good enough. They cannot take that risk.' I looked directly at her. Held her gaze. 'Do you think you can do that if that's what it takes?'

'Yes,' she said immediately. 'If that's what it takes to keep my kids, yes! I *can*,' she added, not convincing me nearly as much as I'd hoped. Not knowing her heart wasn't 'switched off'. '*Course* I can,' she continued. 'My kids come first. They have to. Jake's just … He's … Look, honestly, he *has* changed. He's got a job lined up already, and he's off the drugs. But, like you say, I have to make a straight choice, and I will.'

I wanted to say something – about my experience of the persistent nature of the Jakes in this world. But she was right, I didn't know him. Perhaps he had changed. I hoped he had. I wasn't a giver-upper on people.

And I wasn't about to give up on Jenna. 'You know what,' I said, 'years ago we had a girl called Emma come live with us. She had a brand new baby, and she was in a very similar situation to you, in many ways, though she was even younger than you were when you had Seth – just fourteen. She had another baby, too, and ended up keeping both of them, and she knows what a long slog the process is. She's lovely, Jenna. I think you'd like her, and I know she'd like you. I've been thinking. How do you feel about me putting the two of you in touch?'

She looked immediately suspicious. Another stranger to deal with. 'What, as in *meeting* her? I don't know. I –'

'Not initially,' I said. 'You could meet on Facebook. See what happens. Shall I message her?'

'I s'pose. If you think she would help me.'

'Well, she can't help your case. But she could definitely be a friend to you. Someone who understands what you're going through, at any rate. Someone who might be able to give you some tips and advice. And in the meantime, love, now you've been asked not to by the authorities, it would be much better for your case if you don't have contact with Jake at all for now. Not *at all*. Maybe in the future it's something you can do, and perhaps what you will want to do, if he has changed in the way you say he has. That'll be for you to decide down the line a bit. But *this*, love, believe me, is the fight of your life, and you cannot afford to give anyone any more ammunition to fight you with. Now, let's get these coffees down. We have to be back to school in half an hour.'

And as we sat and drank them, it occurred to me that I too felt in battle. Engaged in the same fight, with someone, against something. But who were the opposition here? And if the answer was social services, then what kind of foster carer was I becoming? Because I was fostering Tommy and Seth, wasn't I? Not Jenna.

It was not a battlefield I wanted to be on. Was pathologically unsuited to being on, just as Christine had warned I would be.

Were her ears burning?

Chapter 16

As a foster carer, I have to say, the best feeling in the world is when you realise that a child who leaves your care takes something of yourself with them. In the early days it's easy to think that you're not making a difference, and to believe that you'll be forgotten the moment a child settles somewhere else, but luckily for me, in a lot of cases that hasn't been true, so I was over the moon when our very first teenage mummy, Emma, phoned me back the minute she received my message.

We had stayed in touch over the years (Mike and I had even been at her wedding) but, as with all our foster kids, it was sometimes hit-and-miss. Birthdays and Christmas mainly (I'm a traditionalist like that), and, of course, if they had any problems. If they'd stayed in touch they knew we'd always be there for them. Which was great – we were always happy to help and support if needed, but equally happy if contact was sporadic due to them having happy, fulfilling lives of their own.

'I've messaged her and she's added me as a friend,' Emma said, after we'd spent a few minutes catching up and chatting about Roman and Mercedes, her not-so-little-anymore little ones. 'And I managed to get her to open up a fair bit. She seems lovely.'

'Ah, so you went all Casey on her then,' I said, laughing. 'Good on you.'

'Of course!' Emma laughed too. 'The apple never falls far from the tree.'

And there it was. That validation. That something, anything, had been carried from me, as a part of herself. It wasn't a smug feeling, merely a contentment deep inside that the work I do does count for something.

'Anyway,' Emma went on, 'did you know Jenna has a court hearing next week?'

I didn't, but that didn't surprise me. It had probably been relayed to her by the solicitor when they'd spoken, but Jenna had been so angry about all the other stuff he'd said that she'd neglected to share the most important reason for the call.

'And as you'll most likely be minding the kids when she goes – I think the solicitor is going to take her to the court – I said I'd meet her for a coffee in town a bit beforehand and go along and support her during the hearing. She was dead nervous, but she says she really wants me to do it. So, yes. There you are. I just hope I can be of use.'

I was stunned – really moved – by what she'd just said to me. That she'd do all that, and for a girl she barely knew.

'Emma, that's *fantastic*,' I said, 'thank you *so* much, love. It will do her so much good to meet you, it really will – to see someone who has gone through what she is at the moment, and come out the other side of it.'

'I did, didn't I? God, it all feels unreal now. Like a dream – lol, no, a nightmare. Not that I'm going to start scaring her about all the pitfalls she might face. Sounds like she's got enough on her plate just now ...'

'You're right,' I said, 'and I think the most important things she needs to hear are that if you follow the rules that social services put in place, to the letter, you keep your babies, and it's really that simple. Did she tell you about Jake though?'

'She did,' Emma admitted, 'and that's the bit that's worrying me, as you can imagine.'

And I could. And all too well – Emma's own journey having been complicated and almost derailed by her attachment to what sounded like a similar sort of boyfriend – the type who gives parents nightmares. Drug dealer. Violent. The usual grim tick list. Cutting her ties with him had been key to her not losing her kids. It was depressing, really, just how familiar and *déjà vu* it all felt.

'What did she say?'

'About him? Not a lot. Only that he isn't the monster "they" are painting him as. Honestly, Casey, it's like we read the same crappy manual. The main thing, as far as I can see, is that whole "them and us" thing. What seems to be preoccupying her the most seems to be working out how she can outwit social services, so she can see him again. She didn't exactly spell it out, but I think she's focussed on that more than anything.'

That seriously bothered me, especially as Jenna had promised me she wouldn't. Had he changed her mind? Did he exert that much control over her? And, as a result, was Jenna's focus becoming less about fighting for her children, and more about beating the authorities who had it in for her? *And* him. I could so readily see that. Yes, she was making the right noises to me – I can't lose my kids. I can't imagine life without them. I'll die before letting anyone else have them. Trouble was that Jenna would also regularly rail against the system, telling me how she couldn't wait to 'shoot those bastards down in court'. Such an adversarial approach definitely wouldn't help her.

Naturally, I'd try my best to impress upon Jenna how she sounded when she spoke like that, how she would come across to the court. But almost inevitably she would be immediately on the defensive, and accuse me of not being on her side, not supporting her. It put me a little in mind of warring parents who, in the middle of an acrimonious divorce, are so busy heaping opprobrium on the adversary they so hate that they almost seem to forget about the effect it might have on the actual children.

There was no question that Jenna hadn't forgotten about her children, but if she couldn't, or wouldn't, stop railing at her 'enemy' I knew she'd come across as immature, reactive and aggressive – none of them qualities they'd be hoping to see in her if she had any chance of getting them on side.

I could only hope that just as a little of me had rubbed off on Emma, so a little of Emma would rub off on this poor beleaguered girl.

Now, however, almost a week after my call from Emma, it was the morning of the hearing I'd heard about so belatedly, and after a largely confrontation-free week, which couldn't help but lift my spirits, everything I thought I knew about Jenna was about to be turned upside down again.

It was 7 a.m. when I awoke and as I glanced at my alarm clock my first feeling was one of instant panic. Something wasn't right. But what? Seth. That was what. He normally started up shouting from his bedroom much earlier – he *was* my alarm clock. Why wasn't he today?

Mike wasn't there. He'd already gone to work without waking me – as he usually did when he was on a run of earlies. Perhaps he'd taken Seth down with him, and now Mike had gone to work, Seth was in the conservatory with Jenna? But sometimes you just have this overwhelming sense that all the options you can think of are the wrong ones. That the silence itself is already thrumming with foreboding.

I plucked my dressing gown from the hook on the back of the bedroom door. If they *were* all asleep still – best-case scenario right now – then we'd be late getting

Seth down to nursery. I opened the bedroom door and immediately almost tripped over, narrowly missing a mug of coffee which, inexplicably, had been placed outside my door. Confused, I leaned down to pick it up. It was warm. Even more confused – who had put it there? – I carried it downstairs with me, full of trepidation. What on earth was going on?

I heard the television before I went into the living room, and entered to see a tableau that blew me away. Was I dreaming? Because little Seth was kneeling nicely by the coffee table, a glass of juice in front of him and a piece of toast in hand, dressed smartly, hair – thankfully grown a little now – clean and shiny, and quietly watching *PJ Masks*. I was too stunned to speak. Seth, however, wasn't.

'Morning, Aunty Casey,' he said, looking anxiously up at me. 'Is it okay that I'm watching the big telly? Mummy needs some time with Tommy just now, so I'm being a *really* good boy. Cos we don't want the social or polices to take us,' he added. Then he frowned. 'Mummy's sad. She's been crying. Can you help her?'

My heart felt as if it had been pulled out and stamped on. 'You *are*,' I agreed. 'You are being *such* a good boy. Please don't worry, darling. You finish your breakfast. I'll go check on Mummy for you.'

The conservatory doors were shut, and I opened them to see Jenna similarly togged up to the max, all ready for her big day in court. She was sitting cross-legged on her bed, in her smart black trousers, and a white tie-necked blouse I hadn't seen before, with her hair neatly straightened, but her make-up all smudged, and, on her lap, Baby Tommy, apparently asleep, who she was gently and rhythmically rocking.

She looked up. And I could see Seth was right – she'd been crying. Was still crying, actually, tears sliding down her cheeks, taking most of her mascara along with them.

'Oh, sweetheart,' I said as I went to sit down beside her, 'don't be scared, love.' I put my arm around her and hugged her bony shoulders, realising just how much weight she must have lost in the last couple of weeks.

In answer she only cried more. 'What's up, love?' I asked. 'Are you frightened about today?'

She leaned down and kissed the baby's head, her hair falling like a curtain. It seemed symbolic, like an act of maternal protection. 'I'm such an idiot,' she whispered eventually. 'I can't bear it. I can't. I can't even bear the thought of it. I don't think I can bear to go on living if they take them.'

Sad though it was to hear, this was music to my ears. To see this genuine outpouring of maternal emotion made my heart leap with equally genuine hope. These were words I'd longed to hear. And Seth had heard them too. I turned to see him standing there, still as a statue, in the doorway. He ran across to us, crying too now, and flung himself on the bed, burrowing his head down under Jenna's arm, close to Tommy's.

'Don't leave us, Mummy!' he said, sobbing, as she put her free arm around him. 'I'll be a good boy. I *promise*.

Every day. I'll be good as good as gold, I swear down!'

'Look,' I said, tears threatening to spill out of my eyes as well now, 'what's happening today is only one part of the hearing. Nothing will be decided, and no one is going to be taken anywhere.' I kissed the top of his head. 'I promise you, sweetheart. Mummy has to go and have her meeting, but she'll be back before you know it, and we're going to have a special tea to celebrate.' I squeezed Jenna's shoulder, and motioned that she should give me Tommy, who I carefully placed, still asleep, in his baby seat. 'And you, my girl,' I added once I'd done so, 'are going to wash that face and re-do that make-up. No, let's call it war paint. Because you are going to put on your game face and be brave, okay? Right, coffee. By the way, did you bring me that coffee earlier?'

Jenna nodded. 'Seth and me thought you might want a lie-in. Since you're going to be looking after Tommy all day, all on your own.'

'And I was really good,' Seth added. 'I was really, really quiet. And I got dressed all by myself,' he added proudly.

They exchanged a glance. And a smile. Now, this was more like it. 'Well, that's *extremely* thoughtful of you. Thank you,' I said.

And see, Jenna? I really wanted to add but obviously didn't. *See what you can do with this little one when you set your mind to it?*

As I dressed, though, I felt a mixture of emotions. Slight regret – this was no time to be talking about war paint, Casey! Plus sadness, because the little family downstairs were clearly in pain, and with a future that must seem so uncertain. But I couldn't help but feel a little optimism breaking through, because that's what this felt like – a breakthrough. To see her cry like that, to see the naked emotion – for a girl who'd been so reluctant to open up about herself, this was incredibly heartening. I could only hope she could convey some of that raw emotion to the judge as well.

Thinking back to how her parents were, I suspected Jenna had built many emotional barriers, and had yet to understand that giving free rein to her emotions would not break her, that it would instead help her heal. And it was doubly – no, triply – important that she did so because, if she didn't, her own babies would suffer the consequences of her broken psyche, whether intentional or not.

But I couldn't help remembering how Christine had chastised me. Was it my job to try and open those doors? Strictly speaking no, because it wasn't Jenna that I was fostering. But morally, yes, I had a part to play in that, didn't I? I might not be fostering her but she was living in my house, and her mental health impacted on the children I *was* fostering. So, yes, I would definitely have to try.

It was a crisp, frosty morning – bitter cold, but with a watery sun emerging, and catching the ice spicules that rimmed hedges and branches and making them shimmer like diamonds. It couldn't help but lift my mood as we set off down the road – as did the evidence that, as a result of a date in a court diary arriving, that bubbling of emotion to the surface Jenna had obviously experienced seemed to be having an effect. I got the strong impression that this morning had been a watershed moment, as not just Jenna, but Seth had reached some kind of understanding of what was at stake here. He walked nicely to school and when we dropped him at his classroom, instead of kicking off, he threw his arms around his mother's legs.

'Promise you'll come back,' he cried. 'Don't let the polices keep you, please, Mummy.'

With Jenna looking as if she might burst into tears again, I held onto the pram handle and squatted down to Seth's level. 'Sweetie, Mummy hasn't done anything wrong, so there will be no police involved. It's just a meeting, that's all. And when I pick you up from nursery, you, me and Tommy will go shopping, so we can choose the things we want for our special tea. Would you like that? Maybe we could even get a cake. You'd like that, wouldn't you, Mummy?' I added, glancing up at Jenna. 'What kind of cake's your favourite?'

'Chocolate!' Seth immediately answered for her.

'No,' Jenna said, seeming to pull herself together. 'That's *your* favourite, you little monkey! Mine's coffee and walnut.'

'But you like chocolate too,' Seth said, as she scooped him up and kissed him. 'I think we should have chocolate. Casey likes chocolate, and –'

'Enough now,' I said, rising to my feet as she put him down again. 'We'll get both. Now off into school with you,' I added, seeing Mrs Sykes approaching. 'Quick kiss for Tommy, then it's time to skedaddle.'

Jenna said little on the journey back home. Which wasn't difficult because the pram meant it was hard to walk two abreast, and if she wanted to be left to her own thoughts, so be it. After her emotional outpouring earlier this morning, perhaps she needed silence to help her mentally prepare. There must be so much going on in her head.

There was little time, once we were home, for a proper chat either, as a taxi had been booked to pick her up at ten, so she'd have time for a coffee with Emma before meeting her solicitor and going into court. It was a quarter to before she emerged from conservatory, hair and make-up refreshed, her flats swapped for a pair of low heels.

She put Tommy's empty bottle down by the steriliser. 'He should stay down for half an hour,' she said. 'Maybe longer if you're lucky.' Then she frowned. 'God, I'm so nervous I could throw up,' she told me. 'D'you think she'll actually turn up?'

'Who, Emma? Of *course* she'll turn up, love. Does your solicitor know you're meeting her? That's she's going in to support you?'

She nodded. 'He knows the café. He said it's practically next door to the court building.'

'I know the one,' I told her. 'I've been there myself.'

'With Emma?'

'Yes, with Emma. And with other kids, too.'

'Your job must be *so* weird,' she said. 'Don't you find it depressing, being around all this horrible stuff all the time?'

'Sometimes,' I admitted. 'But no, mostly not. I –'

'New evidence,' she said suddenly, obviously off on another train of thought altogether. 'He said he'd come get me half an hour before the hearing so he can share any new evidence with me before we go in. What new evidence does he mean?'

'I imagine it might be reports from the children's social worker. About where they're up to in the process,' I told her. 'Or it could even be about the statement your mother put forward. I mean, you haven't actually seen that, have you?'

She shook her head. 'Am I even allowed to?'

'Absolutely you are. You have a legal right to see anything that's to be presented in your case, so it could just be that, and before you start flapping,' I added, seeing her increasing anxiety, 'don't forget that hearsay isn't proof. It's just one person saying something. To which you have the right to reply – to dispute it if it's wrong.'

Jenna frowned again. 'That's the thing. How do I *do* that? I'm so rubbish at stuff like that. I'm useless at sticking up for myself and Mum knows that. She knows I just get all flummoxed and then lose my shit altogether. If they make me stand up and say stuff to try and defend myself, I'll lose it, I *know* I will. I'll probably end up kicking off and getting kicked out of court.'

I took both of her hands in one of mine and squeezed them firmly. 'You absolutely can't do that, Jenna,' I said. 'That's one of the reasons why your solicitor wants to see you before you go into court. He will run through everything he thinks will or might be said, so you know what to expect, and don't have any surprises. And when he does so, if there's anything you don't feel you can answer without getting upset and losing it, then you must tell him you need him to speak *for* you. Give him all your answers beforehand, and don't, *at any point*, be tempted to shout out in court. That's a definite no-no, love, trust me. Bite your tongue and let the solicitor do the work.'

Jenna was silent for a few minutes, while she poured herself a glass of water, then she turned around, and leaned her back against the sink. 'You know they put me on the streets when I wasn't even thirteen yet, don't you?' she said.

'What? Who?' I asked, confused at this sudden turn in the conversation. 'Your parents?'

She nodded. 'Yeah, my so-called mum and dad,' she said. 'Does the solicitor know all that, d'you think? D'you think I should tell him?'

'I have no idea,' I said. 'I mean, I'd like to think they know everything pertinent to your situation – I'd hope social services will have looked into all of that. Or at least tried to. But would they know? I mean, if you haven't told them anything about yourself? When you went to prison, for example. Did you tell them this then?'

She shook her head. 'Why would I do that? They'd taken Seth in for me, hadn't they? If I'd told them they would have taken him off them, wouldn't they?'

Of course they would. So, tragically, this made perfect sense. 'But why, love? Why on earth would they throw you out?'

She rubbed a finger and thumb together. 'Money. I hadn't been going to school because they wouldn't buy me a uniform and all the kids took the piss out of me, so I was just hanging on the streets. Anyway, I got this kind of boyfriend. He was fourteen and had been permanently excluded from his school, so we just, like, hooked up. His mum was a junkie, his dad had fucked off years ago, and you won't believe this but it's true – he lived in the shed in his garden.'

'Are you *kidding*?' I asked. 'Oh my God, that's horrible.'

Jenna shrugged. 'It wasn't, actually. He preferred it. He wouldn't go in his house, except to get clothes or food if there was any, because his mum always had dealers round and men sprawled all over the place, and he had done the shed up lovely – cushions and duvets and stuff. We even had a little camping stove.' She smiled at a memory. 'We'd go shoplifting early in the mornings to get, like, bacon and bread and stuff, so we were fine.'

My picture of the memory she described was

substantially less rosy. *Twelve*. She'd been *twelve*. '*We*?' I said. 'So you stayed there too?'

Jenna let out a little laugh. 'Keep up,' she said. 'Yes, of course I did. And as soon as Mum and Dad realised I had someone else looking out for me, feeding me and that, they told me to fuck off. More money to spend on them. Though they said I had better keep it quiet or I'd end up in a home – they were still carrying on claiming benefits for me, *obviously*. But, you know' – she shrugged, drank some more, and put the glass back down on the counter – 'it was fine. It suited me, I was happy.'

'And?' I asked, trying – and failing – to imagine a twelve-year-old living in a shed with a fourteen-year-old, undiscovered. 'How long did this go on for?'

'About a year.'

I gaped at her. 'A *year*?'

'More or less.'

'And no school?'

'A bit, here and there.'

A bit, here and there. How many times had I heard versions of this? Of serial absconders and truants, and parents who kept their children out of school. And of schools, underfunded, but still trying to do their best – sending letters, making reports, visiting families (*I'd* done that) – but eventually giving up the ghost. 'So it obviously came to an end,' I said. 'How?'

'Winter. That next winter. It was proper freezing. Not like the last one. And Zack – that was his name – was wanting to spend more and more time back indoors.

And I didn't want to do that. He was, like, doing drugs and that by then, and I just sort of got twitched by it all. I mean, I really liked him, but – well, you know. It was just all too horrible. The way some of the blokes looked at me. I didn't feel safe there anymore. So I went back home. I played them at their *own* game,' she told me – and I could hear the pride in her voice. 'Said if they didn't let me stay, I'd ring the benefits place and tell them I hadn't been there for yonks. They didn't like it, but they didn't have any choice, did they? They are arse-holes, Casey. I mean, like, you have no idea what horri-ble, *horrible* people they are. And even worse on the booze by then, obvs. So as always, if I wanted anything, I had to sort myself out.' Another wretched smile crossed her features. 'So, I'd shoplift. And if I came home with a six-pack of cans or a bottle of vodka, I was like their golden child. For five minutes, anyway. *Arseholes!*'

'And the boy, Zack. Did you keep in contact with him?'

She shook her head, glancing towards the kitchen clock as she did so. 'Nah. He hung himself not long after I went home.'

It's hard to articulate how I felt, hearing all that. Sick to the stomach doesn't quite cover it. Not only because of the tragic loss of a young boy, but because of the matter-of-fact way Jenna had suddenly imparted all these horrors to me. As no biggie. Just an aspect of her past that she was musing on, as part of considering if she should fill in her solicitor. As just an accepted part of her life.

'Jesus, Jenna!' I said, and with feeling, because that aspect of it sickened me even more. 'That's *horrific*. Oh my God, love, you must have been devastated.'

'Yeah, I was upset about Zack,' she said. 'That was proper sad. But, you know ...' Another shrug.

I drained the coffee I'd made earlier, that had long since gone cold. 'Sweetheart, have you ever *told* anyone any of this?'

'No, but I will do,' she said emphatically. 'If it looks like the social or the judge, or anyone else for that matter, is about to take anything that comes out of Mum's mouth seriously, then I'll spill my guts about everything. My childhood, the way they've cheated the system for years. My bastard father. *Everything*. I'll get my solicitor to write it all down, so he can show her up in court if he needs to. No one in their right mind will believe a word she says once they know what she's *really* like.'

I was still reeling from what Jenna told me when the cab came and she left. Then I got out my Marigolds. Hopefully I'd have sufficient time to make a proper job of at least Seth's bedroom and the bathroom, and once Tommy was awake again, I could pop him in the sling and do the downstairs with him snuggled up against me. I hadn't felt such a powerful need to attack the cleaning in a long time.

It wasn't so much the story – these kinds of appalling, heart-wrenching tales were par for the course in my fostering life – as was the fact this had apparently been going on for so long, for years, by the sound of it, and *no one had even noticed*. And I only knew a fraction of it. What other horrors were to be revealed?

It also didn't escape my notice that if Jenna had been discovered, and had entered the care system when she was twelve (as she so surely would have), I might even have fostered her myself, well, for argument's sake, anyway, and have been the one in her corner, fighting for her, advocating, as I'd done for many teenage girls before her. Instead, I wasn't even invited to the 'party', in that it wasn't my place to support her in court. To even *be* there. My legal responsibility was to her boys. Children she might not even have *had*, had someone – anyone – noticed her plight, let alone now be having to fight for.

It was a sobering thought. Surely I *had* to help this girl. Starting with a major talk with Christine about them looking deeper into her background. Though not until today's ordeal was over, obviously, and we knew the state of play better.

The cleaning wasn't helping, either. Where, normally, it was a task that pleased and helped me no end, this morning it made me feel even more miserable, as it revealed the full extent of Seth's destructiveness. Which we were, to be fair, already conversant with, as the list of deliberate breakages – the toaster being the latest – was growing on a weekly basis. But this was in some ways worse, because it was all covert. Crayon on walls – but in places he didn't expect me to look, such as behind bedside tables, or the inside of wardrobes. Biscuits and sweets crushed and hidden underneath his bed, and more stuffed toys (some I didn't even recognise, presumably bought by Jenna) ripped to shreds, and thrown into the back of the airing cupboard. So, sadly, his behaviour wasn't exactly improving, was it? He was merely getting better at hiding the evidence of his escapades.

Not having heard anything from Jenna by the time I had collected Seth from nursery and we'd been to get our shopping, I got the baby fed and settled and, after Seth and I had had some lunch, I took over the daily 'Mummy and Seth' time. I was determined this would happen every single day, including today, in Jenna's absence, because he so needed to expend all that energy.

We played *PJ Masks* in the garden, Tommy watching from his baby seat in the conservatory, and by the time all of that was done, it was getting on for four. No news is good news, I told myself nervously but just as I did so, as if by psychic transmission, my mobile screen lit up. It was Emma. 'Mummy! Mummy!' Seth started up. 'Mummy coming home!'

Emma, I thought, answering it. *Not Jenna*. Why not Jenna? But perhaps she'd just left her and thought she'd ring to give me a quick debrief. Which was thoughtful of her because it meant I'd have time to prepare, if the news wasn't positive. And I was right. Because she told me Jenna was indeed on her way home. And after a day that had *not* gone as intended.

Emma didn't mince her words, either. 'It was awful,' she said. 'Utter chaos. That bloody boyfriend of hers turned up in court and started a right commotion. Screaming and swearing at the judge, yelling at her and telling her to give her back her effing kids or he'd punch her effing lights out. He was dragged away by two policemen in the end, screaming that the bloody judge was a paedophile, of all things!'

'Oh, good Lord! And how is Jenna?'

'In a bit of a state, as you can imagine. Though I didn't get much of a chance to speak to her before her solicitor dragged her off. I said we'd catch up on Messenger later.'

'And what about the hearing? How did it go for her?'

'They decided to abandon it. The judge ended it early, gave social services a dressing-down about presenting their evidence late or something, and said it's adjourned for two weeks while she decides what to do. Sorry to be the bearer of bad news, but it was just *awful*. I hope she's okay.' She sighed. 'Well, maybe "okay" is not the word, but you know ...'

That was just it, though. I didn't. What on *earth* had that boyfriend of hers thought he was doing? Was he really that stupid that he didn't understand how badly his actions might have damaged her case? Perhaps profoundly, too. Perhaps beyond redemption.

Almost certainly beyond redemption, I decided. At least as things stood. No sane judge would rescind a care order for two little ones, knowing the mother was consorting with a character like that.

But what could *I* do now to help redeem things?

In truth? Very little.

Chapter 17

Try as I had done to keep my voice down speaking to Emma, Seth had obviously picked up on the nature of what had been said because he was yanking at my top as soon as I ended the call. 'Where's my mummy?' he'd demanded. 'Tell me! When's my mummy coming home?'

I managed to reassure him that she was on her way home, but as the time passed and she didn't arrive, he became more and more agitated, and when he heard the front door open, and it was Mike and not Jenna, he became almost hysterical.

'Where's my fucking mummy?' he screamed at him, as he appeared in the living-room doorway, throwing himself at him bodily and pummelling his thighs with clenched fists. 'The polices have got her, haven't they? They've thrown her in jail! Make them bring her back or I'll have you done in!'

Baby Tommy had chosen that moment to present me with a poop explosion and as I was changing him in the conservatory there was little I could do other than let Mike take over, which, thankfully, he did – he already knew the state of play, because I'd messaged him.

'That's enough!' he barked, getting his hands round Seth's skinny torso, and scooping him up so he had him at eye level. Seth's arms were still flailing, trying to land blows on Mike's face, but he was strong enough to hold him up just out of range.

'Are you going to stop, so I can talk to you?' he now said more quietly. 'Are you going to calm yourself down? Casey's already *told* you. Your mum isn't in jail, she is *on her way home*. Now, you need to stop all this noise and commotion and *calm down*. Can you do that for me, Seth?'

He walked across to the dining table as he spoke and leaned down in front of it, sitting Seth down on the table as he continued to hold him. Seth was having none of it, however, and pummelled his fists against Mike's chest. 'They 'rrested her. I know they did! You're a fucking *liar*!' And with that came the kind of blow no man could withstand; yanking a knee up, Seth then exploded his foot out in front of him, making contact, as intended, with Mike's groin.

Just as Sam Burdett had done before him, Mike couldn't help but buckle, the agony all too obvious on his face as he bent over. How he managed not to utter a few choice expletives himself, I'll never know. Done with the baby now, I put him down on his playmat. 'I've got this,' I said, as Mike staggered back and groaned.

'Right, young man, that is *enough*!' I said, taking hold of Seth in a two-armed manoeuvre, picking him up sideways, facing away from me, as if carrying a roll of carpet. At least that way he couldn't kick me or grab my hair.

Then, somehow, while Mike rode the waves of pain he'd inflicted, I managed to find the strength to bundle Seth up the stairs, where I deposited him unceremoniously on his bed. He was still shouting and crying and threatening to have us shot but without saying a word, I turned around and left the room, shut the door and stood there holding the handle. Though, to my surprise, I didn't hear the immediate 'thud' of his feet hitting the floor and the yanking on the handle that usually followed.

I gave it a minute, even so, and only when that minute had passed did I descend the stairs. If he emerged now, I would simply carry him back up there again. Or Mike would, and I was pretty sure he knew that.

Mike was in the conservatory, in the middle of lowering himself gingerly onto the edge of the little rattan sofa. 'Look at him,' he said, nodding towards Tommy as he saw me approaching. 'Poor kid. What a bloody shambles of a life to be born into.'

I could hear the anger in his voice. 'You okay, love?' I asked.

'I will be,' he said, 'but I'm not sure how much longer we can put up with this, Casey. We shouldn't have to. And it's not just him,' he said, flicking his gaze up to the ceiling. 'It's her too. Sneaking around, texting that ex of hers, when she *knows* what the score is. It's her fault, today. That's the truth of it. *She* caused it. If she'd done as she'd been told to and not had any contact, then the guy wouldn't have turned up in court, would he? And if she took the time to teach that boy a bit of respect, then things like *this*' – I watched him wince – 'wouldn't happen either. And don't even *start* me on our shed being a bloody electrical goods graveyard. Or the fact that I'm going to have to redecorate the whole house when they leave. I'm sick of it, that's the truth of it. Sick of it.'

I didn't know what to say. He was right: it *was* Jenna's fault. No, he didn't know what I knew, in terms of what she'd today disclosed to me, but there was no getting away from the fact that, to *any* observer, it looked like being a mum simply wasn't high enough on her agenda. Not above the world inside her phone. He was right about the mess too – as I'd seen myself during my cleaning stint this morning – and about the number of our things Seth had wilfully broken. At the last count – I mentally ticked off the list – a television, two remote controls, the toaster, our tumble dryer – all in the space of a few weeks. And all pretty much without consequence. On the contrary; Jenna's response when faced with such misdemeanours was more often to squirrel him away in the conservatory, watching telly, eating biscuits, because to her mind, the best way to keep him out of trouble (and, by extension, me from nagging her) was to keep him laid low and out of our way.

Which, to Seth's mind, of course, was a win-win situation, and his behaviour, over and over, was richly rewarded. Oh, it was all so messed up.

And apparently not about to get any easier, because we could hear Jenna's raised voice through the living-room window before she'd even rung the front doorbell.

I ran out to let her in, at least thankful for her timing, now definitely not being the time to get into a justification conversation with my poor husband.

She was in tears. No surprise there. But she was also really angry, throwing a 'Thanks for fucking *nothing*!' over her shoulder at the departing car as she stomped across the threshold.

'Where have you been, love?' I asked. 'We were expecting you back an hour ago.'

'There weren't any taxis,' she said. 'Some concert thing in town. So that dickhead of a solicitor had to drive me.'

'Well, that was kind of him, at least,' I said. 'He –'

'No, it wasn't! It was his fault! If he hadn't made me hang around all that time I could have got a lift with Emma! Anyway, *everything's* fucked up now so it doesn't even matter!'

'Jenna, calm *down*,' I told her, seeing the state she was in. 'Come on, come into the kitchen and I'll make you a coffee. Mike?' I added, raising my voice so he could hear me. 'D'you want a coffee, love?'

'No, thanks,' came the answer. 'I'm going to go up and change.' But I noticed he didn't pop his head round the kitchen door on his way upstairs, and I guessed he probably didn't want to face Jenna.

Which was fair enough. He was too angry. I went to fill the kettle.

'So,' I said, 'I spoke to Emma. She told me about Jake. Did you *know* he was going to turn up in court today?'

This question produced a fresh bout of tears. 'No! And I mean it. Not at *all*. I'm such an idiot. We've only been texting. That's *all*, I swear down. He knew he mustn't do that. I *told* him.'

'So, you knew he wanted to. And at some point you must have told him the date. Jenna, what were you *thinking*?'

'I didn't mean to. And he promised me he wouldn't. He *promised*. Then he just –' She spread her arms then slapped her palms down on the worktop. 'He just does what he wants. He won't take no for an answer. But he didn't mean to cause all that trouble – he really didn't. He just lost it because he loves me. He just can't ...' She sighed heavily. 'He just really *loves* me. And now he's in trouble all over again.'

I pursed my lips. Hard. To stop myself blurting out anything I might regret.

'What happened to the "no contact" thing, though, Jenna?'

She had the grace to look ashamed. 'I wasn't trying to start anything up again, I promise. I told him we were done. That I had to think of the kids. That, Seth or no Seth, there was no way I was going to get back with him.

Ever. That, you know, maybe in the future, he could have some contact or something. He is his father after all, and it's not like he wasn't sending money and stuff for him. And he said he got that. He understood. And I really, really thought he *had*.' She sighed. 'I couldn't just *ignore* him, could I?'

'Love, that was *exactly* what you should have done, hard though it might have been. And I think you know that too. So have they locked him up again?' I added, trying not to sound too obviously hopeful.

Jenna shook her head. 'No, not yet. I mean, he was taken to the cells, but he's out again now. He rang me about ten minutes ago, while I was in the car coming back. He's getting done for assaulting a police officer. The stupid dickhead took a swing at one of them when they escorted him out, but he's out on bail now till his court case next week. He will go back to jail though, for definite. God, back *again*. I mean, I *know* I mustn't see him again. And I won't. But it's still so un*fair*.'

I spooned coffee into mugs, wondering what the hell to do next. Wait, I supposed, for the inevitable calls to ping in. 'And what about *your* court case, love?' I asked. 'Did your solicitor have any idea what will happen with that?'

'My solicitor has no idea about his own *name*. He's useless. But the judge was clear. It was a lady judge – I think the same one from before – and she had to stop the proceedings with all the Jake stuff. But she at least said I couldn't be blamed for his outburst, and she's set the date for another hearing – in two weeks, I think. But she did say she would look very dimly on me if I have further contact with him. God,' she said again, 'he's *such* an idiot.'

I poured the water into our mugs and mused on her idiosyncratic tone – her ability to say the word 'idiot' in this context and manage to make it sound indulgent – even loving. Even now, I didn't trust that she'd completely seen the light; it felt more like, now he'd come in, all guns blazing, to court, that she owed him. At least needed to help him. I wouldn't have been in the least bit surprised if she secretly found his behaviour heroic. Her one true love, pitching up to fight her corner. Which in itself was hardly unreasonable, was it? She had no one else in her corner, after all.

'So,' I began, handing Jenna her coffee, 'now we need to regroup – think about how to prepare for the new hearing. I think –'

'Mummy!'

I turned around to see Mike and Seth had appeared in the kitchen, the latter being carried, with his arms now outstretched. Mike set him down on the floor. 'Someone wants to say sorry,' he said. 'Go on then,' he added.

'I'm sorry, Casey,' Seth said. And he looked like he meant it.

'Apology accepted,' I told him, as he ran into Jenna's arms.

'I thought you'd been 'rrested,' he told Jenna as she reached down to pick him up.

'No, you silly billy,' she said. 'I just couldn't get a taxi. But I'm here now. So, has my best boy been a good boy today?'

Marginally, I thought, as Mike and I exchanged glances. At least slightly better than the other 'best boy' in her life. At which point, Jenna's phone, out on the worktop, let out a trill. 'Shit,' she said, glancing at it. 'I mean, oh dear.' She looked at me. 'Forgot to tell you, Sam Burdett is on his way round.'

So not Jake, at least. But Sam Burdett? 'What, now?' I said, thinking about the special tea that wasn't. The special tea that wasn't even on my radar any more. As wasn't any tea, not if I didn't do something to change that. And it was already getting on for six. 'Why?' I asked. 'To follow up on today?'

Jenna shook her head. 'He wasn't even there. Some other woman from the social showed. I don't know who. Lizzie something? But I didn't even speak to her. It's not to do with that, he said he had to come for his statutory visit or something? He said it's the law that he has to see the kids today.' Hmm. Nice of someone to let *me* know, I thought. 'He said it wouldn't take long, though,' she finished. 'Fifteen minutes and then he'd be off.' She waved the phone at me. 'That was to say he's on his way.'

Great, I thought. Great. All we needed right now, being just at the point when it would have been useful to get the little ones fed, bathed and down for the night, so we'd be freed up to have some useful conversations with Jenna about the revelations I'd heard earlier in the day. As it was, my hackles rose slightly. They couldn't seem to help it. It just seemed so obvious that the last person to throw into the mix, under the circumstances, was Sam flipping Burdett. Who would, I was sure, even if his visit wasn't related, be up to speed about what had happened in court today. And would doubtless bring along his own opinions.

'Right,' I said. 'In that case, I think we'll do a re-jig on tea. Have a takeaway once Sam Burdett's been and gone. How does pizza sound? Mike, will you text Ty and see what he'd like?'

'Pizza! Pizza! Pizza!' Seth whooped delightedly, looking for all the world as if the stormy scenes earlier (both here and in court) hadn't happened, and that everything, once again, was all right with the world.

Which is children's special gift, I thought, as I finished my coffee. That magical ability to live totally in the moment – something us adults so often strived to, but failed.

I was failing right now. Badly. Because I had this premonition.

That much bigger storms were massing just ahead.

Chapter 18

Given that Sam Burdett would be on our doorstep in less than half an hour, I broke with protocol and volunteered to give Seth his bath so that Jenna could concentrate on feeding Tommy and getting him ready for bed. In the big scheme of things it was hardly a criminal offence, I reasoned. She'd had a long and stressful day and the last thing I wanted was for him to turn up on the doorstep and see us all frazzled. He was the one who'd chosen tonight to turn up, after all.

It also meant Mike could enjoy a precious half hour watching the news uninterrupted, which felt only fair. And Seth, perhaps knowing he must rise to the occasion (or perhaps just because there was a pizza carrot being dangled), behaved in an exemplary fashion, chatting away to me about all his PJ Masks superpowers, and sniffing all the lotions and potions along the side of the bath, putting them in categories of 'nice' and 'ugh-disgusting'. I'd never known a kid, I mused, with such a sensitive nose. And when I brought him down again, clean and fragrant in his hero's pyjamas, he even went over to Mike, without prompting from me, and apologised a second time for kicking him.

So, it seemed the stage was set for at least a civilised encounter, and when Jenna emerged from the conservatory, having put Tommy down, she too seemed a great deal more calm. Still, when the doorbell rang, I felt the same sense of foreboding. There was little doubt in my mind that Sam would know all about today's debacle, and trying to convince him that we mustn't completely give up on Jenna just yet felt like one heck of a mountain to have to climb.

Jenna decided to settle Seth in the conservatory with Tommy, out of earshot of any discussions we'd be having but with the door slightly ajar, so still in sight.

'Just keep calm, love,' I told her, before I went to let him in. 'Remember, losing your temper is going to count against you so, even if you feel like it, bite your tongue, okay? This is just a stat visit – a legal thing. A box-ticking exercise. And if Sam wants to discuss anything about what happened in court today, keep your cool. You have a new date and a new chance to go before the judge, and, remember, *you* didn't do anything wrong today.'

But then I clocked Sam Burdett's expression. I barely knew the guy, but some expressions are universal. This guy had the bit very much between his teeth and for reasons that I'd have loved to be able to sit down and discuss with him, looked like he was keen to be out of the traps and cantering down the home run. Could it be something as simple as him having made up his mind from the outset that he didn't like Jenna?

Needless to say, when I ushered him into the living room you could almost hear the atmosphere crackle.

'Jenna, Mr Watson,' he said, nodding as he greeted them, then casting his eyes around as if wondering what we'd done with the children. Which might not have been the case but Jenna picked up on it immediately.

'They're in there,' she said, swivelling to gesture to the conservatory. 'Tommy's asleep and Seth's watching the television. Is that good enough for you? Or do you need to go in and check they have pulses?'

Her tone wasn't lost on him – just as I imagined she'd intended. And no amount of me counselling calm and restraint was going to stop this angry young woman making her feelings clear. And perhaps in cautioning against that I had in fact made it worse. I hoped not.

'That won't be necessary,' Sam said, a flat tone to his voice now. 'Now, if we can get started.'

'Right,' Mike said, 'I'm going to leave you all to it. Unless you need me, that is?'

'No, no,' Sam assured him. 'Just Casey will be fine.'

I was pleased about that. I didn't want Mike to be part of it. Yes, he'd made his feelings clear about the toll things were taking, but equally, he'd always had a strong nose for bullies, and I could already sense he was sniffing the air.

Perhaps, being fair, it wasn't all Sam Burdett's fault. He'd been passed on information about the debacle in court, and could only respond to what he'd been told. But right away it was clear that this was going to be no normal statutory visit. Stat visits were usually upbeat and positive – a chance for the social worker to touch base and have a catch-up, and to discuss anything that might need discussing. But there was no getting away from the fact that in this case Sam wasn't seeing the two children who formed part of his caseload but the mother who he'd already made clear – even if not explicitly – that his department felt not up to the job of looking after them. Perhaps that was at the heart of it; that social services were having to manage a situation that, had the judge not intervened in the first place, they would not have to be managing.

I'd also done my sums and wanted to put my marker down. Was this a stat visit or wasn't it? 'Sam, it's not quite six weeks yet, is it?' I asked him. 'I wasn't expecting to see you till next week.'

'Not quite,' he replied, 'but six weeks is the minimum. And I had to come over anyway. Because of what happened in court today.' He smiled humourlessly at me. 'Two birds with one stone. And yes, I know I wasn't there.' He glanced at Jenna as he said this. 'Unfortunately I had too many prior commitments, but my colleague Lizzie has debriefed me about it, and –'

'What prior commitments?' Jenna asked. 'Why am I not a priority? This date was set weeks ago, wasn't it?

And how could someone who doesn't know anything about me speak up for me?'

At which point I caught Sam's expression and I knew I must brace myself for the worst.

'Jenna,' he said, sounding horribly patronising, 'it wouldn't have mattered who was there from our side, to be honest. Because, as you already know, as does Casey, because you were told this from the outset, we are all of us singing from the same song sheet.'

I felt the temperature of the room, already chilly, plunge to freezing.

'What does that mean?' Jenna asked. 'What's he trying to say, Casey?' she added, turning to me now.

Sam immediately raised a hand to stop me from answering. 'It means, Jenna, that our position hasn't changed. It's up to you to prove to *us* that our preferred course of action isn't the right one. Up to *you*. And what happened today was, well –'

'I didn't do anything wrong! I showed up, I dressed smart, I was ready to answer questions. It wasn't my fault what happened. It wasn't me who kicked off!'

Her voice was becoming shrill, so I put a hand on her arm to try and centre her. The last thing we needed was for Seth to barrel in, and if she raised her voice any further, I felt sure that would happen.

'No,' Sam acknowledged, 'but the man who *did*, and is only just out of prison, is your boyfriend, and you don't need me to tell you that your relationship with him is the single biggest factor against you right now. You were told not to contact him. That was something you agreed to.' (Another thing, I noted, that I'd not been made aware of. There had definitely been no '*Jenna must not contact Jake*' on that sheet we'd been given. No mention of him at all. Talk about going in blind.)

'I didn't *ask* him to go there and *there is no relationship*! Or are you saying I'm not allowed to send a text message to *anyone*, *ever*, for *all time* – is *that* it?' She was getting really angry now.

San shook his head. 'Jenna, please don't be flippant.'

She leapt from her chair then. 'Flippant? You think I'm being *flippant*?'

'Sit down, Jenna,' I said levelly. 'Come on. *Please*. Just sit down.'

Thankfully she did so, though Sam didn't help his cause any by adding, 'That's better.' But perhaps his real cause was being served all too well.

Visibly deep breathing now, Jenna then turned to face him. 'Why don't you stop pussyfooting about and tell me the truth?' she said calmly. 'Go on, spit it out. What are my chances of leaving here with my kids? Do I have any chance at all?'

Sam Burdett cleared his throat and sat a little further forward in his seat. 'If you really want the truth, Jenna, then here it is. Our intention – that is, the local authority's intention – is to apply for both children to be adopted, not fostered.' I gaped at him. Why had I not been told this? But he ploughed straight on. 'Because that's what we feel is in their best interest. Given that there are no suitable family members who we could place them with long-term, we believe that placing them with a loving adoptive family is the only suitable option now.'

I watched Jenna's eyes fill with tears. 'Are you *serious*?' she said. 'Are you fucking actually serious?'

I was stunned. Not by Jenna's reaction – boy, I could well understand that – but by the matter-of-fact way that a qualified social worker had just delivered that kind of news. And he *was* a social worker, so of course Jenna was going to believe every word of it. But I knew, or at least I was pretty sure I knew, that he was wrong, utterly wrong, to make such claims.

I glared at him, and at the same time gripped Jenna's hand and squeezed it. 'Okay,' I said. 'Let's all just calm down for a minute. Sam, I'm sorry but I'm quite sure neither you nor social services are the ones with the power to make that kind of decision. Not in this case. Not when it's already been agreed that it's a judge who is the one who is going to decide on the outcome of this case. I also think it's important' – I glared again at him – 'that Jenna knows this.'

He had the grace to look down then, and start shuffling his papers. 'That's as may be –' he began, but now it was my turn to stop *him*.

'Jenna, love,' I went on, 'it doesn't matter what recommendation social services put forward. Because that's *all* it is. A recommendation. The judge has all kinds of options at her disposal, not just adoption, and it is *she* who will make the decisions here. Please don't get upset. After the day you've had,' I added, as much for Sam Burdett's benefit as hers, 'this is the last thing you need to hear. And remember what I said: it's the judge who will decide. Anyway,' I added, letting go of her hand and returning my gaze to Sam, 'if there's nothing else, I think we should draw this stat meeting to a close so we can start thinking about having some tea.'

Sam clearly agreed. 'Yes, we're done,' he said stiffly, gathering his paperwork and standing up, too flustered himself now to meet my eye as he did so, while Jenna, across the table, just sat and stared at him.

'Good,' I said. 'And I'm sure you'll be in touch in due course. In the meantime, I'll keep filing my reports.'

He couldn't get out of the door fast enough after that, only pausing on the doorstep to turn around and frown at me. 'Sorry about that,' he said. 'I should have handled that better. I can see things are a little bit unsettled here at the moment –'

'Yes, you should have,' I said.

He didn't stop to argue.

I went back into the living room, seething. A little bit unsettled? Zero points for insight. He'd come in like a one-person wrecking ball!

'Well,' I said to Jenna, anxious that damage limitation was the order of the day now, 'I'm glad I never offered him any of your coffee and walnut cake! I'm so sorry, Jen, he should never have said all that to you, even if he does think that himself. Like I said, he can write as many reports as he likes, but it's the judge who decides. *Only* her.'

Jenna sighed, heavily. 'I know. I do know that. But what chance have I got if that's how that bastard feels?' She checked herself then. 'I'm sorry for swearing, but he really upset me. Adoption? I mean, seriously? They mean to put my babies up for adoption? No chance for me to get them back *ever*? God, I can see it all now. This whole mum and baby placement, this "golden opportunity", is just a joke. It always has been, from the get-go. It's just so they can say they tried it – that's the truth of it, isn't it?'

Mike appeared then, in the living-room doorway. 'Jesus!' he said. 'He left in a hurry.' He raised a hand. 'Don't worry, I heard most of it. Couldn't not.' Then he grinned. 'But it sounded like you girls handled it pretty well.'

It was the best thing he could have said and the right time to say it, and even better that he mouthed a choice expletive at Jenna – which looked suspiciously like what I would have called Sam Burdett myself, had I not been such a consummate professional. It broke the tension, too, and enabled Mike to add his own reassurance – that the fight was not over – and she went back off into the conservatory to check on the little ones with at least something approaching a smile on her face.

'Anyway, let's order that pizza,' Mike finished. 'I'm ravenous.'

'So are we,' came a voice from behind him, in the hall. Mike spun around, to see Tyler walk into the living room, home from work. And behind him, smiling shyly, stood Naomi. 'Did you not read my text?' he added, seeing my shocked expression.

'No, love,' I answered, trying to rally at warp speed. *We*. He'd said *we*. So had he brought her round for tea? As in *today, of all days*? Oh, God.

I smiled back. 'But how *lovely*!' I chirruped.

Chapter 19

Fortunately – and perhaps sensing it would be a good moment to do so – Naomi excused herself, saying she needed to use the loo, which allowed me a few moments to bring Tyler up to speed with the situation.

'Ah,' he said, cottoning on to the tension immediately. 'So, not the best timing then. Look, it's fine. Why don't I just tell Naomi there's a bit of a crisis going on? We can just as easily nip out for food instead.'

'Absolutely not,' Mike said, saying exactly what I was about to. 'We've been looking forward to meeting her, and it will be a nice distraction for Jenna, and this is supposed to be a special tea party, after all. And between you and me,' he added, lowering his voice a little, 'I'm not about to let some trumped-up little squirt from the council derail our day any further. Just don't worry if Jenna seems a little stressed, okay?'

So, pizzas were duly ordered, drinks made and the table laid – I even whipped up a salad so Naomi didn't think we had a veto on healthy food. Then I nipped in to tell Jenna that Tyler and his girlfriend would be joining us for food, hoping that Mike was right – that it would stop her brooding in the conservatory, and her angst about everything transmitting straight to Seth.

And, once the pizza had arrived, and Seth appeared to be rising to the occasion, I was even beginning to put it out of my own mind and relax.

'So, Naomi,' I said, smiling to myself at the way she and Tyler kept looking at each other, 'what is it you do? I think Tyler did tell me, but I've got a memory like the proverbial sieve.'

'I'm working at the leisure centre at the moment,' she answered, 'but in September I'm starting university. I'm going to train to be a teacher,' she added shyly.

'Oh wow!' I said. 'Is it primary or secondary schools you want to teach at?' This girl was definitely more than just a pretty face, then, I thought. She had ambition. Just what I wanted for my Tyler.

'Primary school,' she said immediately and then cast her smile towards Seth. 'I love little kids. I never had any brothers or sisters, only my little cousins, so I've always wanted to work with them.'

I smiled at Seth then too. 'Did you hear that, sweetheart?' I asked him. 'Naomi is going to be a teacher, just like Mrs Sykes. You like Mrs Sykes, don't you? Seth's really enjoying nursery,' I added, to Naomi. 'He's settled in really well there, hasn't he, Jenna? In fact, he got a special award for being kind, only yesterday.'

Jenna, who'd mostly been a listener up to this point, rather than a contributor, blushed and cleared her throat. Then, to my dismay, I saw her eyes welling with tears. Oh, no, I thought, perhaps this had been a mistake after all. What must she feel like, being faced with this bright, confident young woman? Inadequate, obviously. On every level.

Naomi, sensitive, perhaps, to the complicated situation, tried to steer attention back to Seth. 'Wow,' she said, 'that's brilliant, Seth. What was the kind thing you did?'

But Seth was clearly sensitive to the situation too. 'Shut up, lady!' he shouted at Naomi. 'You've made my mum cry. Go away!' Then, to my horror (and surprise, since I didn't know he had it in his hand), he launched something across the dining table at her. Which hit her, before bouncing back onto her plate. It was a small metal van.

'Ouch!' she said. 'That hurt!'

Then before she could make light of it – something I was pretty sure she was about to do – Tyler chipped in.

'That's *very* naughty!' he snapped at Seth. 'Apologise to Naomi!'

Upon which, to my even greater horror and dismay, Jenna jumped up from her seat. 'How dare you speak to my son like that!' she yelled at Ty. 'He's only a fucking baby! How would you like me to get all in your face and scream at you? He didn't mean it, for fuck's sake!'

'Jenna!' I said. 'There's no need for that. Seth shouldn't have thrown his toy. He knows he shouldn't.'

'It's okay, Mum,' Tyler said, his face now a mixture of anger and embarrassment. 'No need for you to get involved.' He then looked at Jenna. 'If you don't want him told off, then you should control him better, shouldn't you? You okay, babe?' he added, turning back to Naomi, who now looked as if she wanted the ground to swallow her up.

'I'm fine,' she said, 'really. I'm sure he didn't mean to hurt me.'

'*You okay, babes?*' Jenna sneered. '*God.* Seth, come on. Let's leave everyone to their *nice family tea* and go back into Mummy's room.'

'Jen,' I began.

'But I want to eat my pizza!' Seth whined.

'NOW!' she snapped. He didn't argue. Simply slithered off his chair, a slice of pizza in hand, and followed meekly in her wake.

'Honestly, Mum, that girl's a *nightmare*,' Tyler said, as the conservatory door slammed behind them. 'I'm sorry, but she is. It's her fault he behaves the way he does.'

I felt sick. I could hardly explain to them the extent of what had happened today, could I? The court, the solicitor, her ex, that bloody social worker. I could fully understand why Jenna had been at tipping point, but at the same time, I didn't want to sound like I was making excuses for her behaviour. So I held my tongue.

'I know, love,' I said instead. 'Are you sure you're alright, Naomi, love? I'm so sorry. All I can tell you is that we've all had a really bad day and, well, Jenna isn't dealing with it very well.'

'I'm fine, Casey, *honestly*,' Naomi said. 'It was more the shock of it than any pain.' She reached out for Tyler's hand. 'I'm *fine*, babes,' she added, to a still obviously angry Tyler. 'Forget it ever happened. As your mum says, it's obviously just been a bad day for her. Let's finish this gorgeous pizza, yeah?'

I smiled at her. What a generous spirit this girl had. Despite everything, I was happy we'd had this opportunity to get together. There was nothing to hide now, either – she had seen our house in full-on messy fostering mode. I picked up a triangle of pepperoni and did a mock cheers to her chicken and pineapple.

Tyler and Naomi didn't stay for long once we finished our food; they were off to some party, then sleeping over at Denver's, so I cleared up while Mike gave them a lift there.

'I don't envy Denver's parents,' he said, once he'd returned. 'I had to make a stop at the shop on the way and saw the booze stash Ty came back out with. I bet there'll be some sore heads in the morning.'

I laughed. 'Oh, to be that young again,' I said. 'I remember those days, love, when every night was a party night, but we all still got up for work the next day. I don't know how we did it, do you?'

Mike groaned. 'I do, and, speaking of which, has Jenna come out yet?'

I shook my head. 'Not yet. I did put my head round the door after you left but all three of them were blotto. Hardly surprising, given everything, so I didn't disturb them. I'll try again in a bit – we'll obviously need to get Seth up to bed. And how about you?' I added. I knew Mike had a big stock take in the morning. 'Don't you need to get some shut-eye yourself, love? You need to be in by half six, don't you?'

He nodded. 'Ugh! Yes, I do. If you're sure?'

'Course I'm sure. I'll just give her another pep talk. Make sure she's okay. Reassure her that we can put today behind us.'

'Can we, though?'

'*Yes!* Seriously, that Sam Burdett was talking out of his proverbial. I don't know what his problem is, but he has clearly not read the manual. He had absolutely no business saying any of those things to her. And I shall make that very clear in my report tomorrow morning.'

'But she did have contact with her ex. There's no getting around that.'

'Yes, but only to tell him it was over. Anyway, it's not the point. Sam Burdett didn't even *ask* her. Just dropped his bombshell without so much as asking her a single thing about it, let alone giving her a chance to explain. Which he'd no business doing anyway, because it's the judge who'll decide. And if she keeps doing what she's doing – as in caring for those little ones – and she sticks to what she's said about not seeing her ex again, then she still has a chance. She has a *right* to a chance.'

Mike kissed me on the forehead. 'Of course she does, love. I just hope she doesn't throw it away.'

They were Jenna's kids. That was the bottom line. Her babies. Her flesh and blood. Yes, she'd messed up, and the authorities had been right to step in then. But the judge had decided to extend her that lifeline, so she, and only she, had the power to cut it off. I knew I needed to impress that upon Jenna more than anything, because she could so easily give up hope when hope wasn't yet lost.

I knocked gently on the conservatory door and waited. I could hear the TV burbling away quietly in the corner, but then a barely audible 'come in'.

Seth was on his mother's bed, curled up, snoring softly, and Tommy was fast asleep in his crib. Jenna herself was sitting on the little sofa, feet tucked up under her, reading through what looked like official paperwork. She put it down when she saw me and half-smiled, half-grimaced.

'I'm so sorry about earlier,' she said. 'I feel awful. I just lost it. I didn't mean to. It just suddenly came over me, this massive feeling of anger. And regret, I suppose,' she added. She'd clearly been thinking – a lot. 'I had no business taking it out on Tyler the way I did. I'll apologise to him – and his girlfriend – as soon as I next see them. I think it just hit me – that contrast, you know? How they don't seem to have a care in the world – even if I know that's probably *not* true – whereas I … I just can't get it out of my head now. That in a few weeks, maybe less, they'll just come in here and *take* them … And I'm supposed to just *let* them? Could you? I just don't think I *can*.'

I sat down beside her on the sofa. 'Sweetheart, I promise you, what I told you earlier is true. What Sam said about adoption is just *one* possible option. I can't tell you that it isn't, because then I'd be lying to you. But there are *other* options. Remember, that's *precisely* why you're here with us. To prove to the judge that in this case adoption's *not* the best option. That *you* have what it takes to bring up your children. So if you keep her onside and keep doing things right, she'll have no reason to go along with *their* suggestion, will she?'

Jenna smiled wanly. 'I know,' she said. 'And thanks for the vote of confidence. It means a lot to know that at least *someone* has my back. And you're absolutely right – sod him! I know I mustn't let him get to me. And I'm fine,' she added firmly. 'Just tired.'

'Yes, you need to get some sleep,' I said. 'Shall I take Seth upstairs for you?'

She shook her head. 'No. I think best not to wake him. He'll only scream the place down if he does and wake Mike up. I'll keep him down here with me, if that's okay?'

'Of course,' I said. 'You're right. Let's let sleeping dogs lie, eh?' I stood up, then bent down to place a kiss on her forehead. 'Night, night, then, sweetheart. I'll see you in the morning. New day, new start. You'll feel better once you've slept.'

And sleep I did; for the first time in weeks, I drifted off feeling peaceful. I don't know why – we were still in one unholy mess, for sure. But for all the rows and confrontations, and that bloody Sam Burdett, it felt as if we were getting somewhere. That I was getting to know Jenna. That I was beginning to understand her.

That I'd finally breached her barriers.

What a fool.

'Casey! Casey!'

I woke up with Mike looming over me, shaking me by the shoulder. And the urgency in his voice made me sit up immediately, in that way a 4 a.m. phone call tends to do.

'What's wrong?' I said, trying to blink away the darkness. 'What's the time?'

'Half five. They've gone, Case. She's packed up and left!'

'What? Who?' I asked, trying to unscramble my still-sleepy brain. Then it hit me. 'What, Jenna? What – the *kids*?'

I reached for the lamp switch, squeezed my eyes shut against the brightness, then opened them to see Mike hoicking my dressing gown off the back of the bedroom door. 'Yes, all of them. I double-checked. She's left everything tidy –'

'Did she leave a note?'

'Not that I could see. The pram's gone as well,' he added, handing me my dressing gown. 'I've got to go, love. I'm sorry. But you need to make some calls.'

'No, no, it's fine,' I said, scrambling out of bed. 'You get off to work, I'll deal with it. God, Mike, where could she have gone? It's the middle of the night still!'

'To her parents? To Acapulco? To her flat, perhaps? Your guess is as good as mine, love. I'll call you in an hour or so, once I've got the lads sorted, but now I really do have to go. Get on the phone, love, okay?'

New day, I thought. New start, I thought. Damn.

Chapter 20

I first made a coffee, to wake myself up, and, having woken up, felt immediately frantic, grasping for any explanation I could conjure that wasn't immediately, totally damning. Which was hard, because there wasn't one, was there? But maybe, just maybe, Seth had woken up early, and Jenna, not wanting to disturb the whole household, had decided to take them all out for a walk. Which, I reminded myself, she was not allowed to do. But if she had … oh, please let it just be that.

Which thought had me thinking less edifying thoughts. Yes, Jenna might be very streetwise, but as a family they were vulnerable. Both in social service speak and in every way possible. So, I should ring her. Before doing anything else, I should ring her. So, I did so. And though it rang – which was at least a small comfort to hang onto – that was all it did – rang and rang and rang and rang.

I should text then, I decided, so I hammered one out. *Hi Jen, love. Where are you? Did you go out for a walk?*

Then I waited for a response, refreshing my phone screen repeatedly. The message had been read. I could see that immediately. But there was no bubble to indicate she was typing a reply.

I tried again. *Jen? Please text back, love. At least put my mind at rest. You're not in trouble, not at all. I'm just worried, babes. xxx*

Again I waited. Again the message was read but ignored. Real panic began to set in then. Because, clearly, this was no early morning stroll. *As if it ever would have been, you stupid woman*, I thought wretchedly. She had taken off. She must have. Wasn't the evidence overwhelming? So might she have decided to take her chances with her parents, after all? I just couldn't see it – but then, what did I know? And she'd surely know it would be our first port of call.

Or her flat, perhaps. Might she have taken them there? Might she have got it into her head that she needed some space? But again, if she went there, she would easily be found there. The authority was even paying her rent for her.

So where had she gone? And what did she hope to achieve? Did she really think she could just disappear? Perhaps yes – she'd been invisible to social services as a teenager in a *shed*, for goodness' sake. So she was well used to falling through cracks. Perhaps she'd simply decided to risk it, and hope that she could do so again, rather than run the risk that her social worker *did* hold all the cards. I could have cheerfully throttled Sam Burdett right then.

I went from room to room, looking for clues to where she might be, but only finding evidence that she had left. Empty drawers in Seth's bedroom, missing toothbrushes in the bathroom, half the baby paraphernalia in the kitchen absent without leave, no phone charger, no hair straighteners, no formula, no sling ... By no means everything, but by no means nothing, either. There was nothing for it, it seemed, but to face the grim reality. She'd planned all this, hadn't she? That was why she'd wanted to keep Seth downstairs with her last night. So she could creep around, gathering things up, knowing he was safely downstairs. That, with him down there, she'd run much less risk of us being woken up.

And I'd slept like the bloody dead. Played right into her hands.

There was nothing else for it. There were calls that needed making. Damning calls that needed making. And I was just about to make them – I had the numbers in my contacts – when a message pinged in.

It was Jenna.

I'm sorry, Casey. I had to leave. I don't think I have a choice. Do what you have to, it's too late now. Thanks for everything. I mean it. x

Jesus Christ! So she really was – she was doing a runner. But to where?

I could have wept. Except I couldn't because I was

way, way too angry. Of all the *stupid* things to do. What on earth had possessed her? Knowing my only course of action now would be to call the authorities, to report that she'd absconded with the kids *I* was fostering. With the children *who'd been entrusted to my care*. To put the ultimate black mark down against her.

But did *she* properly understand that? Would that have even crossed her mind? One last chance. One last opportunity to stop her case becoming a train wreck.

It ISN'T too late. Not if you come back. Where are you? Just let me know and I'll drive and come and get you all. If you don't then I'll have to call the police and report the children missing. I won't have any choice. Please just let me know where you are, love. I can give you fifteen minutes to think this all through, no more xx

Within seconds my heart leapt, as the message showed as read, and the little bubble with the dots in started blinking. And then plummeted as it came and went, three times in total. But no message came. Was she tussling with her conscience? Weighing up the risk of absconding with her children, knowing that, as they were children in care, the police would assuredly be on her tail? And how was it stacking up in her mind, given what she thought she *did* know? Given that she'd decided – because there was almost no doubt that she had, now – that she was almost certain to be losing them anyway?

I could have wept. It was the worst kind of Hobson's choice imaginable. And she had been right to ask the question – how *would* I feel if I were her? How would I feel if I had to stand there and watch my children being taken from me? Would I even be able to? To physically let it happen? I didn't think so. And it was so easy to forget, since at no point had it ever even been discussed, she had been parted from Seth once before. How had she felt when she'd been taken to the cells?

I had no answer. To either my question or my text, and all too soon fourteen of those fifteen minutes were over. One last shot.

Jenna, love. Please, please don't do this xx

And an instant reaction.

Two emojis. One of a gust of wind, the other of a map. Was that supposed to mean she was disappearing?

It hit me like a truck. Was it even from her? Would she be that cryptic? That dismissive? That sarcastic?

Oh, God. Was *Jake* with her?

Police first, as per procedure. Which, of course, took for ever, the dispatcher needing a rundown of everything that had happened prior to them going 'missing' – full descriptions of Jenna and the kids, and the pram, then another raft of questions about what might have prompted the disappearance – had we had an argument? Had she indicated she might harm herself or the children? Might she be in 'cahoots' with another party or parties? Did I have any further information I could give them? So I told them about Jake, about the texts, about the scene at the court, and once they'd punched the numbers – or whatever it was that they did – as if by magic, his identity appeared.

'Ah, here the fellow is,' the dispatcher said. 'He's down as one of her known associates. And, from what you've told me, now in breach of his bail conditions, too. Grand. We'll get back to you as soon as we have any news.'

The next phone call wouldn't be so straightforward. Not least, I knew, because it was already gone seven. And, as I'd expected, the EDT (Emergency Duty Team) worker was abrupt; no doubt coming to the end of a busy night shift. I could hear him typing as I spoke, committing everything to the record, and, just when I thought the call was coming to an end, he then began interrogating me anew.

'So you say your husband noticed them gone at 5.30 a.m.?'

'Yes, that's right.'

'And it's now almost, erm, let me see, seven fifteen. Is there any reason for this delay in reporting?'

'Well, I obviously phoned the police first, which took half an hour.'

'Still. That leaves over an hour still unaccounted for. Over an hour of travelling time, which could mean the girl getting some distance away. In any direction,' he added pointedly.

'Yes, I see how it looks, but I did have my reasons. I was in contact with Jenna during that time, as I said, and was obviously hoping I could persuade her to return. It's not like I just sat around waiting,' I pointed out. 'I was trying to avoid a worst-case scenario.'

'But, in fact, Mrs Watson, that's exactly what we *might* have. Anyway, thanks for your call. Someone will be in touch.'

I ended the call and let out an audible groan. I was such an *idiot*. Of course I was going to be in trouble for this. I'd done it again, hadn't I? Given Jenna the benefit of the doubt when I absolutely shouldn't have. Not after the last time. And it wasn't like I hadn't been warned about it. By my own husband, whose first action on finding them gone had been the right one. Why the *hell* hadn't I just done what I was supposed to?

I felt tears prickling at my eyes, but refused to let them fall. What business did I have blubbing out of what was essentially self-pity? *Suck it up, Casey!* I thought, as I stomped back upstairs. I had brought this on myself, and I would just have to face the consequences. I'd taken on a placement that Christine had told me, *and in no uncertain terms*, that I probably shouldn't have. That I didn't have the cool rationality to deal with. Yet I had. And now I'd proven myself wanting. It didn't matter an iota what I thought about it, either. No impassioned plea from me would make the slightest bit of difference. I had given Jenna, in my naivety, an unacceptable window of opportunity in which to get away. Why hadn't I allowed myself to believe she'd have gone with Jake? Why hadn't that been the very *first* thing I'd thought of?

I also had less than hour now, I judged, before the offices would open, my masters would assemble, and my phone would start bleeping and dinging like a telephone exchange. I needed to get showered, get dressed, get my sh** together, basically. I had an onslaught coming, and I needed to be ready for it.

And come it did, in a tidal wave of recriminations, large and small. No sooner had I put the phone down on the school – whose absence line I'd called, to let them know Seth wouldn't be in today – then in came a call from Mike. Who at least kind of understood my reasoning – though for entirely different reasons. He was more shocked that the dodgy, out-on-bail ex-boyfriend would even have the resources, or the desire, to take on two small children, much less the wherewithal. But I still had to listen as he voiced his amazement that I hadn't immediately got on the phone after he left for work. He knew I already felt bad, so he didn't make a big thing of it, and in fact tried to make me feel better by telling me that my instincts were always second to none, that the fostering team knew this, so he was sure everything would be okay. What he didn't say, at least, was 'I told you so'. Because though I deserved it right now, I couldn't bear to hear it.

Then came Christine, who must have had her ear to the ground, because she already knew all about the absconding.

'My God, Casey,' she said, 'this isn't going to do the girl any favours when she's back in court.'

'I suppose you've heard that I was late reporting it too?' I answered. 'But, Chris, in context, it's not half as bad as it probably looks on paper. I was working on the assumption that she'd absconded alone. Had I thought for a moment that her ex might be behind it, I'd have got on to the police before doing *anything*. And as soon as I did, that's exactly what I did do.' I stopped then, suddenly aware that what I'd just said to her sounded even *worse*, perhaps, that it might look on paper. How naive did I sound? *Why* hadn't I considered it? 'Am I in big trouble?' I finished.

'Look, Casey, I can absolutely see how you were thinking, but, truthfully, I don't actually know. There's to be a meeting tomorrow to discuss all this with managers, so I'll have to let you know after that. But there's no doubt about it, an experienced carer such as yourself is expected to be fully conversant with the protocol. Which I know you are, normally. And I sympathise, genuinely.' She paused for a second before continuing. 'Perhaps this placement has, well, maybe just knocked you a little off-kilter.'

She wasn't being patronising. That wasn't Christine's style at all. But her words made me feel even worse. As did her follow-up – that, assuming they caught up with Jenna, which she was confident would happen, we would have to face a 'return home' interview. With Sam Burdett.

'One horror at a time,' I said. 'And by the way, re Sam Burdett, I'm not saying this just to try to make things better for Jenna, but the way he spoke to her yesterday [had it really only been yesterday, I thought?] was completely out of order. He told Jenna the children were going to be put up for adoption. He used the word "intention". Said it was the authority's *intention*. Not "suggestion", but "intention". And he didn't make any attempt to soften the blow either, or show an iota of empathy. In fact, after a day that had already been extremely stressful for her, he seemed determined to trample on any single thread of hope left in her. I'm not trying to let myself off the hook, Chris – this is strictly between you and me – but I'm absolutely sure that's a factor in what's happened.'

There was a long moment of silence. 'Noted,' she said finally – and after such a lengthy pause that I wondered if she'd literally made a note. 'And listen,' she added, 'don't beat yourself up, okay? This was always going to be a difficult placement. This whole family were an unknown quantity, and in so many ways, and it's not like you've just muddled through. You've gone out of your way to help them, every step of the way. Everyone knows that. Look, okay, so you made a bad decision this morning, but I think we've all been guilty of that one time or another. Please try not to worry. I'll be in your corner tomorrow. Anyway, let's hope they pick them up soon. I'll call the minute I hear anything, okay?'

I wasn't quite sure what to do with myself then, rattling around my empty house, waiting. It wasn't even nine yet, the day barely begun, but it felt like I'd been on a treadmill of hard labour already.

I'd been here before. And more times than I could count on my fingers. And every time I experienced the same set of emotions, from frustration, to anger, to sadness, to guilt. And every time came the inevitable wave of sheer terror. Because one day, I was sure, every single time it *didn't* happen, that the call I received wouldn't be from a cheery police constable, to announce that we could stand down, that they had the child or children, that all was well. It would instead be a sombre-voiced senior police officer, to let me know something terrible had happened.

So now, when my phone trilled, I had the usual spike of fear: was this time going to be that time?

The display, however, didn't say 'No caller ID'. It said Jenna.

I swiped to answer. 'Oh, thank God you've got in touch!' I said. 'Where are you?'

I could hear a lot of background noise. Outside noise. The baby crying. 'I don't know. A place called Harborough, or something? Market Harborough? I've just got off the train.'

'The *train*?'

'The train to London. I don't know what to do. I just thought I should get outside the station – get away from here – in case he comes back on another one. Another train.'

'Jake's not with you?'

'No, we got off when he went down to the buffet. What should I do? Should I call the police? I'm scared to hang around here in case he comes back and finds us. Seth, *shut up!* You can see I'm talking to Auntie Casey! Or should I see if I can get a taxi? I'm right by the rank. Oh, God, I'm so *sorry* ...'

I could tell she was panicking, distressed, struggling to speak. Casey, *think. Market Harborough.* Where was that? Many miles away. Maybe even a hundred or more. Lord, what time had they left to get so far away? And *how?* And, much more to the point, how to get them all back again? 'The police,' I said, decided. 'Call 999. Immediately. Tell them who you are, and where you are. You're already in the system, and with the kids being with you, they'll send someone out to pick you up right away. Then go and wait for them, somewhere safe, around people. If there's a café nearby, I suggest you go there. Go on – do it now. I'll –'

'I'm *so* sorry, Casey. I just –'

'Now,' I said again. 'Call me afterwards.'

I was shaking, I realised, proper, full-on shaking, my fingers skittering across the screen as I pulled up my recent calls, to let the local police know I'd had contact with Jenna. This time they were quicker. Not exactly warp-speed, but at least no list of twenty questions. They'd liaise with their colleagues and make sure they were in touch. 'Don't call her yourself, though,' the dispatcher said. 'Just text her. Because we'll obviously want to keep the line free.'

I did as asked, sending a text to let her know the police were on it, to which I got a reply straight away. *They're*

coming to get us. Jake's ringing and ringing though. So I'm
going to turn my phone off. I'll switch it on again when we're
coming. I'm so sorry. Xx

I could only hope sorry wasn't what we'd *all* be.

The police car pulled up at around eleven, and I went to
the door to meet them. Seth was first to jump out and he
immediately ran straight to me, holding his arms out in
front of him to be picked up.

'I've been in a police car!' he told me excitedly as I
scooped him into my arms.

'So I see,' I said. 'How exciting!'

'And McDonald's. And a train.'

'Oh, I'm *so* happy you're back, baby,' I said, giving him
a tight squeeze. 'Now, shall I put you down so I can help
Mummy with Baby Tommy?'

Seth nodded, and then gave me an unexpected kiss on
my cheek. 'Can I go watch the big telly in the room for
being good?'

'Course you can,' I said, setting him down. 'Go on,
you know how to put it on.'

I'd expected Jenna to look embarrassed but as I went to
help her get the pram from the police car, I could see she
just looked awful. Tired, distressed, weary, sad. All right
there on her face and in her body language. She looked,
more than anything, so slight, and so *young*. I felt very sorry
for her. Much more sorry than annoyed at what she'd done.

But proud, too, that she'd acted the way that she had.
Not only that, she'd had the sense to realise what she

249

was doing, what she was risking, but also to act – and so incredibly decisively and bravely. I just desperately wanted to know what had happened.

'There's no need for me to come in,' the police officer said, smiling. 'Jenna's given us a statement, and they've all been fed and watered, so I'll get off if that's okay, unless you need me for anything?'

I shook my head and thanked him before following Jenna into the house. She was carrying a large rucksack, her handbag, the baby and his changing bag. I had the pram and Seth's little school backpack. Not very much stuff, I thought, with which to start a new life. I took the baby from her arms so she could take off her coat. Was that really what she'd thought she'd been doing?

I flicked the kettle on with my free hand while Jenna made up a bottle for Tommy. After my early start, and the anxiety that went with it, I felt wired, but at the same time, now all the adrenalin was subsiding, I knew I'd better top up before it all started catching up with me. I was also conscious of the time. Before I knew it, the cavalry would be here, in the shape of Sam Burdett, wanting to do his 'return home' interview.

'So,' I said, the baby still nestled in the crook of my arm, 'while you feed this one, how about you tell me everything? Starting from when I left you to go up to bed. Was that when this began, or was it earlier?'

Jenna popped the made-up bottle in the microwave and set the timer for her usual fifty seconds. Then turned around. And I could see from her expression that she was going to be frank now. She'd crossed the Rubicon now, hadn't she? So she might as well be honest.

'Before that. We were texting – *not* in the way you're thinking. I meant what I said yesterday. I wasn't lying to you about Jake. I knew – I *know* – he's the last thing the kids need in their lives. He was just telling me about how he knew he was going straight back to prison, so he'd be out of my life anyway, and that he was sorry, that was all. And, I don't know, I just ended up telling him what Sam Burdett had told me, and Jake was sorry about that too, because he *knew* he'd fucked it up for me. And that was kind of it, till he told me he could at least help with money.'

'Where does he get all this money from?'

She gave me a sideways glance as she pulled the bottle out of the microwave, slipped her cuff up and tested the temperature on the inside of her arm. All unthinkingly. Just routine. Just one day after another of doing all the little baby things. Unthinkingly. Automatically. No big deal for many of us, but this was a girl whose only experience of babies, as far as I could tell, was the one she'd had herself, at just fifteen years old, after spending her early teens with another kid, living in a shed. And soon after that, as she'd put it herself, f**king up, big time. Put like that, put in context, her performing these simple everyday maternal tasks was actually a very big thing indeed.

Jenna took Tommy from me, and lowered herself onto a kitchen chair. 'Where do you think?' she said simply. 'Anyway, I told him I didn't want his money. That I was going to lose the kids anyway. And it sort of grew from there. I just …' She frowned. 'I just couldn't see a way out. So when he suggested we do a runner, it just, I don't know – you know what it's like when you're lying there in the dark and everything feels hopeless … It just, well, at the time it just seemed to make sense.'

'You surely didn't *really* think you could just disappear off into the sunset? Jenna, you're not stupid. Far from it. You must have *surely* known that. For one thing, the pair of you both have criminal records. And for another, you had two little ones in tow.'

'I don't think I *did* think. Not beyond running away, anyway. It just felt better than doing nothing. Better than just waiting for my future to be decided for me. I just had this really strong need to escape. No offence to your conservatory, Casey, obvs,' she added, smiling, 'but it's been so horrible cooped up in there every day, knowing I couldn't even leave the house with my own kids without permission. I s'pose I just wanted to be on my own with them. In charge of them. Looking after them. Not –'

'On your own with them but with Jake,' I pointed out.

'God, no! That was never in my plans. That was just what *he* thought – he had this mad idea that if we got to London we could get the Eurostar and go to France …'

'Without passports?'

'Not right away. He had a mate somewhere down there who he said we could stay with till we could sort something out.'

'Seriously?'

'He was dead serious. No way was he going back to prison if he could help it. And he probably could. He probably will. If they don't catch him, that is. You forget, he's done stuff. He knows stuff. He's older.'

'How old?'

'Twenty-nine.'

I did some quick maths. So, at the age of twenty-five, he'd got a fifteen-year-old pregnant. No, maybe even a *fourteen*-year-old. I had no words for him at that moment. Well, not that I could say out loud. 'So what was *your* plan, then?'

'I didn't have one – I really didn't. I just thought if I could get to London … I don't know. Honestly. It was like I was high on something. I just wanted to get out. Run away. Haven't you ever wanted to run away so bad you can't think beyond it? No, you probably haven't, have you?' she added, before I could answer.

'A couple of times. When I was young, maybe, and had got into trouble. But, no, not like you. But, love, I *get* that. I understand. So, you decided you'd go with him. What then?'

'He arranged to pick me up. He had a friend who said he'd drive us to the station. Not round here. To where we could get a fast train to London. So I crept around, got some stuff together – I was totally on board with the whole thing now. I was *buzzing*. So that's what we did.'

'At what time?'

'Around half four this morning.'

That brought me up short. This was still the same *day*. 'You must have been like a ninja,' I said. 'Seriously.'

'Believe me,' she said, setting the empty bottle down on the table. 'I am *very* good at being quiet.'

For reasons that would probably depress me, I decided. 'But we didn't even hear the car,' I said. 'And our bedroom's at the front.'

'Lol, it was electric,' she said. It made us both smile.

'So you drove to the station, got the train ... when did your change of mind happen?'

'Almost right away,' she said, smiling down at the baby. 'When this one started kicking off. Seth was sleeping on Jake, and he was nodding off as well, and the more I tried to shush Tommy, the more he started whinging, and there was a man on the train, in the seats the other side of us, in a suit, and he kept looking at me as if I was some useless piece of shit ... And I realised. I thought, God, yeah, he's absolutely fucking *right*.'

'So you decided to get off at the next station?'

Jenna shook her head. 'No. Not right then. I got Tommy to settle. And I just sat there looking out at all the countryside whooshing by, thinking how the hell I was going to get us out of this mess. Then Jake woke up and he said he'd head down to the buffet to get us coffee. And juice for Seth because now he'd started kicking off as well. And Jake said he'd take him. Stretch his legs and that. And Seth really, really wanted to. He thought the whole thing was like this massive holiday, of course. And I said no. It just hit me that he mustn't go with him.

Which made him kick off even more, but I stayed firm. I wasn't having it – lol, you'd have been *so* proud of me – and I gave Jake some line about how he wouldn't be able to keep hold of Seth *and* carry the coffees, so off he went, and even then I hadn't actually made a plan yet. But then they said the next stop was going to be that station, and I knew the buffet car was, like, *miles* down the train. And the train was filling up now, so it would probs take him a while to get back. And it just suddenly hit me. We should just get off. Get our stuff together and get off the train. And Seth was, like, why? And I told him it was our stop, and he was, like, yeah, but what about my dad? And I made up some nonsense about him having to stay on till the next stop to get a car from a mate – which thank God he swallowed – and that was that. We got off. And I phoned you.' She stood up slowly, and gently lowered Tommy down into his baby seat. Then, rising, she looped a strand of hair over her ear and sighed. 'And now I'm back, and I suppose I have to face the consequences.'

It was Jake, however, who was first to have to face the consequences; they were relayed to me by Gilly Collins on the phone not long after Jenna got back. There were police ready and waiting to pick him up at St Pancras. Where he compounded the offence of breaking the terms of his bail by head-butting one of the constables. So, back to prison, and hopefully for a long time – and well out of the reach of Jenna. But, at least on that front,

I had a hunch – a hopeful hunch – that the ties had already been cut.

But Jenna was all too soon forced to confront her own reckoning, as along with the news that Jake had been re-arrested, came the less edifying news that Sam Burdett would be with us within the hour.

'So what you have to do now, love,' I told Jenna, 'is keep your cool, absolutely. Just tell him what you've told me and don't lose your temper with him, even if he provokes you. And I tell you what. I'll mind the little ones so you can get a bit of shut-eye. A little power nap, shall we say – because you look like you need it.'

'Seriously, I could sleep for a week,' she said with feeling.

'You have twenty minutes,' I told her. 'Set your phone timer.'

Though, as it turned out, Sam Burdett didn't arrive for a good ninety, citing some contra-flow system on the A-road near the office, by which time, having changed the baby and played polices (oh, the irony) with Seth for a bit, I'd taken him up to bed for a much-needed sleep. Though, as it turned out, Jenna hadn't been using her own nap time to nap. Instead, when I popped my head round the conservatory to tell her he'd arrived, she emerged with a couple of sheets of A4 paper.

I'd made Sam a coffee – I felt ill-disposed towards him, obviously, but not that ill-disposed – and, having established that both boys were, indeed, home, and apparently well, he'd taken up his place at the dining-room table.

Jenna placed the sheets, which I could see were covered in tightly packed writing, down in front of him. 'It's all there,' she said. 'Everything I told to Casey, it's all there written down for you. So I don't have to go through it with you all over again. Feel free,' she added, nodding towards it. 'I'm just going to get myself a glass of squash.' Then glancing at me and smiling grimly, she left us to it.

Sam picked up the sheets and began reading, as instructed, going 'hmm' once or twice, and, at one point, nodding to himself, while I gently rocked the baby seat on the floor beside me.

'Well,' he said, once he was done, 'this is certainly comprehensive.'

'So what now?' I asked.

'So I take this away and file it. She's not –' He paused then, as Jenna returned with her drink. 'I was just saying to Mrs Watson,' he continued, 'you've not done yourself any favours with this escapade, have you?'

Jenna didn't sit down. Instead she shrugged. 'What difference does it make? You already said you were intending to put my kids up for adoption. What worse thing than that can you actually do to me? Have me shot?'

I didn't like the way this conversation was proceeding. But at the same time I couldn't help but admire her for saying that. I was also torn. What I absolutely mustn't do now was give him any reason to think I was acting as her advocate. But it didn't appear that she even felt she needed one.

'I'm going to fight you, by the way,' she said, her tone low and level. 'I'm going to fight you with every single breath in my body. I'm going to fight you till I don't have a breath *left* in my body. Just so you know. Anyway, do you have any more questions? Because I need to go and wake Seth up. Not good for kids to sleep for too long in the day, or it's impossible to get them down at night. You probably know that.'

Her barb wasn't lost on me. And, I didn't think, on him. 'I think this will be enough,' he replied. 'Unless you have any questions?'

'Nope,' Jenna said. 'Not that I can think of at the moment.' She looked at me. 'I'll go up then, if that's okay?'

I nodded. 'I do have some questions,' I said, once she'd left. 'I take your point about this "escapade", even if I don't happen to agree with it, but are things really that cut and dried now? That adoption is, in the view of the authority,' I added pointedly, 'the only outcome on the table here?'

Sam slipped Jenna's papers into the folder in front of him. 'I can't see that the judge has any other choice after this, can you?'

'But aren't there other options? I mean, is it *really* so that it's either adoption or she gets them back in a situation such as this? I'm not an expert, but I'm almost positive that's not actually the case.'

He shifted in his seat. 'Well, yes, hypothetically, there are multiple options. One of them being that they remain in a mother and baby placement for further assessment, for up to a year. But that obviously wouldn't be under consideration in this case because Jenna's already proved she can't be trusted and stick to the rules, even when under strict observation.'

I bit back on my urge to insist that he qualify that statement – at least to cite me specific examples, *in this case*, where we could at least open up a conversation. Where I'd have an opportunity, while obviously acknowledging her lapses in judgement, to cite examples where she had demonstrated some pretty sound maternal judgement – and against a background so awful, such a lack of any role models, that, in this case, they were pretty damned impressive.

But I mustn't do that, I knew. So I simply kept prodding. 'You said multiple options. So what else might the judge look at?'

'Long-term fostering, obviously, while the mother appeals. Though that's not what we're recommending –'

'Any others?'

'Yes,' he said, and I could hear the exasperation in his voice. 'But none that the authority are recommending.'

'But don't you have a duty to explore all the options? These are her children we are talking about and she is desperate not to lose them.'

'First and foremost we have a duty to those children,' he said. 'And for that reason we are clear what our recommendation is going to be. It is in the children's best interest to be adopted straight away. I know you think you know this girl better than I do and want to fight her corner, but it would be even worse for them, particularly the baby, to be in the middle of a long, drawn-out process, only to be taken away in the end.'

Sam's words stayed with me long into the night as I tried to decide what to do about what I'd heard. On the one hand, I could see that Jenna lacked many parenting skills, but she clearly loved her babies, and she was learning, wasn't she? And did her lack of skills at the moment mean that she automatically deserved to lose them? Not in my eyes. In my opinion Jenna was as much of a victim as anyone in this case. She had been severely neglected herself as a child and had slipped through the net. The authorities hadn't chased her down. Schools had simply stopped sending truancy letters home and had assumed the family had left the area. Nothing had been followed up, leaving poor Jenna without role models, without anyone, in fact, to show her what real parenting was all about. I tossed and turned till I finally drifted off to sleep, and when I woke at dawn, I knew what I had to do.

I had to fight her corner.

Chapter 21

The following day, Jenna was staring at me open-mouthed across the breakfast table, Seth next to her, stuffing Sugar Puffs into his.

'So, what you're saying is, social services have been holding back the truth from the judge?'

Before we'd sat down for breakfast, I had casually let slip to Jenna that I'd been doing some digging, which I had, into the various options that in fact were available to her. And that adoption wasn't the only alternative on the table if she didn't win her case outright. She must have been mulling around in her head what I'd said and had just taken what she wanted from the conversation.

'No! I didn't say that,' I said. 'Please don't say I said that, love – I'm in enough trouble as it is!'

Seth giggled. 'Auntie Casey, your mouth is like an O. O for octopus.'

This was a thing with him currently. In every shape he found a letter. Now he was in nursery, he was coming on really well with his alphabet. Whereas, I reflected, he would have started with V for vodka if he'd still been languishing with his grandparents, for sure. 'And your chin is all M for milky,' I told him. 'Now that you've finished your cereal and been a very good boy, you can go and have fifteen minutes' TV before we get ready for school, so I can talk to Mummy, okay?'

He didn't need telling twice. He jumped down from the table and scurried off.

'But they have, haven't they?' Jenna said. Which I supposed was fair comment.

'No, because the judge will already know there are other options. But it's like anything in court, there's two sides to the case. On the one side, there's social services, who make their recommendations, and on the other there's the lawyers who are acting for you. And what I'm saying is that I really think it's worth speaking to your solicitor and asking him to ask the court if the various options can be explored, in the event that you don't outright win your case.'

'Which you don't think I will.'

'No, love, I don't think you will. We both know that's unlikely, but what *isn't* a given is that the children will automatically be put up for adoption if you don't. You have every right to ask him, and he should put them forward.'

'And what are they then?'

'Well, there's fostering, of course – that was the initial thinking, as you know. Which would mean you had regular contact visits with the children and could in time start the process of trying to get them back again. Then there's the option that they stay in care, so they are legally not yours yet, but living with you instead of a carer. Though, to be honest, I suspect that's highly unlikely, given everything. Then there's the option of an extension to the current assessment period, where we carry on doing what we're doing for a period to be agreed.'

'You'd do that?'

I nodded. 'We'd do that.'

'But don't you want your life back?'

It was a thoughtful, perceptive question. Because yes, yes, I did, and if we did go down that road, I'd be kissing it goodbye for a while yet. Though, curiously, when I'd discussed it with Mike the previous evening, it had been me who'd been dithering, not Mike. In fact, he'd said yes immediately. We were in it now, he'd said. We had a duty to see it through.

'It's fine, love,' I told her. 'It's not quite conservatory weather, is it?'

She nodded, looking thoughtful. 'So I should tell him that, should I? That I want him to put all that forward to the judge, and because he's working for me, so to speak, he has to do what I say, right?'

'Sort of,' I said. 'But, love, please don't ring him up all guns blazing, and being all demanding. We get the best results by using sugar, not salt.'

Jenna laughed. 'Oh, Casey, you are funny,' she said. 'I

don't know what the hell you're talking about half the time, but I swear down, I'll be nice. I'm going to ring my brief as soon as we're back from nursery.'

And she thought I sounded funny? Ring her brief indeed; she sounded like some kind of little gangster! But 'ring her brief' she did, the moment we got back from the school, and forgetting all I had said about taking the softly, softly approach, she did exactly the opposite and demanded her solicitor start up new paperwork immediately and put a new application forward. 'He's on the case,' she informed me when she emerged from the conservatory. 'Lol, and he really is, isn't he? D'you think that's where it comes from?'

'That's exactly where it comes from,' I agreed.

In reality, however, this was nothing to do with me. I was fostering Seth and Tommy and what happened to Jenna now would only be my business if the court case went for her and she was granted the second chance she so needed. In which case, as we'd agreed, I would knuckle down and see it through.

But I was no less agitated by the uncomfortable nature of my role than I'd been when I'd agreed to plunge in. One thing was clear, after this, though – I would not be doing any more mother and baby placements. They'd been fine twenty, or even ten, years ago, but these days they took too much out of me. Not physically so much – I'd been pleasantly surprised on that front – but the emotional push and pull had been exhausting. And so much harder than I'd imagined – and I'd imagined it would be hard – because I knew that if Jenna lost her kids to adoption I would spend the rest of my life feeling terrible about it, because you can't live with someone, specially someone so disadvantaged by the circumstances of their birth, and not want to help them. Not if there was anything you could do to help them. And in Jenna's case, I genuinely did think she had a fighting chance of being a good enough mother to those boys.

And, of course, in acting on that impulse, that instinct, I was once again going to get my knuckles rapped.

The call came from Christine just after lunch, while Tommy was dozing and, since it was raining, Jenna and Seth were absorbed in some construction job at the dining table, with my craft box.

'It wasn't nice, Casey,' she admitted, after the usual 'How are things?' 'At first they were all talking about ending the placement there and then. Moving the kids to another foster carer and telling Jenna she would have to go elsewhere.'

I was aghast at this. 'Seriously?'

'Seriously.'

So, a tad more than having my knuckles rapped. I listened in silence as Christine explained how she fought my case in a rather tense meeting, citing how far Seth had come on with his behaviour in the last few weeks, and how she felt it would be detrimental to his development were he to be moved again. But there was no getting away from it, she explained to me gently. Their faith in my judgement had really been shaken.

'I know that,' I said, 'and I completely understand it. In all my years of fostering, I've never hesitated like this in such a situation, and that's why I had hoped that managers might understand that these were a really unusual set of circumstances.'

'Which they were,' Christine went on, 'and that's why everyone decided to allow the placement to continue, but it doesn't alter the fact that whatever the reasons behind it, the children were at risk. I know absolutely that you desperately wanted to give Jenna the benefit of the doubt, I know that. But there were others in that meeting who even brought up the possibility of collusion ...'

'Seriously?' I interrupted. 'After what Sam Burdett said to her, that feels a bit rich. What about the part he played? Because I truly believed Jenna had reached the end of her tether after her argument with him. And I couldn't blame her, either, not the way he spoke to her. God, I wish I'd noted that in my report now,' I finished.

Collusion. I hated that word and it made me feel sick. It had only been said to me once before and that was years ago when I was fostering Emma and Baby Roman. One social worker had accused me of covering up risky behaviour by Emma because I had become 'too close' with her. Here we were again.

Christine was quick to jump in. 'It was said in a written statement *by* Sam Burdett. He didn't attend the meeting, by the way. He's actually handed in his notice. He's decided – surprise, surprise – that social work isn't for him. He's using up his annual leave till his end date. And don't worry – I know you didn't want me to include it, but I felt it was my duty to let everyone present know how he spoke to her. Not in mitigation of your actions, just as an aggravating factor in hers. Anyway, it's all academic now. I'm not sure he's been in the best of places, to be honest. I don't know the details, but I suspect he's well out of this kind of work.'

Which made me almost feel sorry for him. He always gave the impression that it was all a bit too much for him, but to throw in an accusation like that before he left made me feel angry, and not at all sorry for him.

'Good.' I said. 'I never felt he was right for the job, and I cannot believe he thought I was colluding with Jenna. It's absolutely ridiculous. Look, Chris, what do I have to do to move on from this? You know I made a mistake and I accept that, but I don't want it hanging over me.'

She laughed down the phone. 'I have that covered already, Casey,' she said. 'My manager has accepted that so long as we reflect on this at your next review, and you complete a refresher course before then on risk management, then you'll have ticked all the relevant boxes and we can move on. End of.'

So I accepted my dressing-down, and what I had to do to make things right with as much grace as I could muster, but before Christine got off the phone, I wanted to know about the next social worker, because the children would definitely need one.

'Good news on that front at least,' she said. 'It's going to be Lizzie Croft. I think you've already met her – she was the one who brought Tommy to you from the prison? I know she's been doing some family support work, but she's actually a social worker too. She was taking a year of doing part-time, which led her to the role she's been doing recently, but she's agreed to come back full-time and take over Sam's role and so there it is. New social worker for Seth and Tommy.'

That did lift my mood, pretty considerably. I had liked her instinctively, and I trusted that instinct. I also felt sure she'd build a really positive relationship with the children. And Jenna too, which was something that really mattered.

Well, *might* matter. There was still a major hearing to get through. And, without question, given the stern words I'd heard earlier, there was a high chance that Jenna could still lose.

Chapter 22

Before any of us had time to get our heads around it, it was the day before the court hearing and we were all beginning to feel it. And to compound Jenna's anxiety, I took a call at eight in the morning from Mrs Sykes, Seth's teacher, who'd requested a meeting.

'What can she want?' she demanded, 'and why would she ring you and not me? *I'm* his mother, aren't I?'

'For goodness' sake, calm *down*,' I said. 'She would have called me because it's my number she has, isn't it? And – a small point this – you were in the shower.'

'But what about? God, he's not in trouble, is he? If he gets chucked out of this place, that's going to look terrible on my record.'

'She didn't say, so stop jumping to negative conclusions. She just said she'd like to have a quick chat with us about certain aspects of Seth's behaviour.'

'So he *is* in trouble.'

'*No*. She did not say that at any point.'

'But why did she say "us", and not "me"?'

'Love, she didn't mean anything by it. Right now, we're a unit in law, you and me. It just is what it is. Stop getting your knickers in a twist!'

And right now, I didn't add, Mrs Sykes had to follow protocol as much as me. And I was the one with parental responsibility.

'Anyway,' I hurried on, 'shall we nip into town with Tommy this morning and get you a new top for court tomorrow? There's also a bit in the budget going begging, since you've bought so much for the boys yourself, so maybe we can get a couple of other bits for you too.'

It worked like a charm, her angst immediately forgotten. 'Can we go to Next? I saw a gorgeous black hoodie online last night. I was going to order it too. But I thought, no, Jen, save your money in case it all goes tits up in court, and you have to make a fast getaway with the kids again.' She looked at me and laughed out loud. 'Joking!'

I sincerely hoped she was. About the getaway, *and* the hoodie! 'Come on then, chop, chop,' I said to Seth. 'Let's get you ready, because we have to be in school early. Mrs Sykes wants to let you into the classroom before any of the other boys and girls get there. What a treat that will be, eh?'

Seth nodded sagely. 'She probably wants to let me build a jail to put the bad kids in. I'm good at that.'

'Well, perhaps not quite that,' I said, but he was not

to be dissuaded, and when we arrived, he announced that was exactly what he thought he should do.

'Yes, of course,' Mrs Sykes said. 'That's an excellent idea, Seth. I'll be at my desk talking with Mummy and Auntie Casey while you do that, and then we'll all come and take a look once it's finished.'

'It's always a jail,' Mrs Sykes said to me and Jenna once he'd gone over to the far side of the classroom. 'Can't ever be a den or a shop or something nice. Always a jail, or a cell or a police station. Goodness knows what some of the other parents must think when their children go home and say they get arrested every day!'

Jenna looked anxious. 'Is that what he's in trouble for? Is that why we're here, because I swear down he doesn't get any of that stuff from me. His nan and grandad used to always be telling him about his dad being in jail. I promise it wasn't me.'

Mrs Sykes shook her head. 'Goodness me – not at *all*! I love it when he uses his imagination through play, and he's so funny with it – he often has us both in stitches. No, he's not in any trouble. Not at all.'

'Well, that's a relief,' I said as we all sat down – Mrs Sykes on her desk and Jenna on the other chair, while I perched on the edge of the nearest table. 'But I'm intrigued now. What's going on?'

Mrs Sykes explained that she and some other staff had been monitoring Seth closely, after witnessing some of his odd behaviours. Such as the way he treated Jenna and I before going into the building – the screaming and aggression – but then how he changed the very instant we were out of sight. He apparently had some strange ways in class too. 'I don't know if he does this at home,' Mrs Sykes said, 'but he sometimes deliberately takes things that belong to other children and squirrels them away out of sight.' Jenna looked glum again, but Mrs Sykes smiled to reassure her. 'Then he always seems to monitor them – watching as they discover that the thing is missing, and then making a big thing out of "helping" them to find it – their shoe, or their comforter, or whatever it is he's taken – telling them not to cry and that he'll try to help them find it, then eventually leading them to where he "thinks" it might be. And it's more than him seeing himself as the hero,' she added. 'We thought that at first – that he was trying to gain peer approval. But it seems a little more complex than that. It's almost as if he's conducting mini-experiments – trying to understand other children's reactions, their emotions. We've also found him more than once seeming to practise expressions. In the wavy mirror, over there – things like sadness or anger. As if he's learned them and is trying them on for size. He's also hyper-sensitive to loud noises and to smells. Have you noticed that?'

'So basically, you're saying my son's a nut job?' Jenna asked, though not at all defensively. She sounded genuinely interested. 'I mean, he does do stuff like that at home, doesn't he, Casey?'

I nodded. 'He definitely squirrels things away,' I said.

'And you're right about his sense of smell. He often comments on how things smell, doesn't he, Jenna?'

'All the time,' she agreed. 'He gets really agitated when I'm changing Tommy's nappies. What's that down to, then, do you think? What does it mean?'

I thought back to previous children I'd had, and their various idiosyncrasies, and also, of course, to Kieron, who was on the autism spectrum, and could have written the idiosyncrasy handbook.

It was Jenna who continued though. 'Does it mean he's autistic? There's a girl I'm friends with on Facebook and her son's autistic. They have to put noise-cancelling headphones on him when they go out to the park because he freaks out if he hears a plane going over.'

It was a thoughtful contribution and I was pleased at her engagement. I sat back a little to let Mrs Sykes talk directly to her. 'It's too soon to tell,' she said, 'especially as he's only been here for a very short time. But the reason I asked you here was to tell you that I think it would be helpful to refer Seth to a child psychologist, so that they can explore what's going on in there a little further. It might be multi-factorial – it probably will be.' She glanced at me. 'I know he's had some challenges to face, and they will obviously have impacted on him, but we're of the mind that there might be something else going on. That he might have other challenges.' She tapped her temple. 'With how his brain's wired, if you like. The only problem is that because he's obviously still very young, they may want to wait until he starts in school before investigating further. However – and of course I know he will most likely be leaving here soon – I still think it's worth getting him into the system, so to speak, as I think it might be helpful for you, moving forwards. Because, trust me, I know how difficult it is to get a foot in the door when you need that kind of help. What do you think?'

'I think fine,' Jenna said. 'I'll use all the help I can get with him.'

'Ditto,' I added. 'Absolutely.' I turned to Jenna. 'And this *will* be a great help, I'm sure. You've always said Seth can be a handful, haven't you? And it's so easy to assume it's just because he's had environmental challenges to cope with. But if it *is* more than that, it –'

'Will prove to the social,' Jenna finished for me, 'that it's not *all* my fault.'

'Exactly,' Mrs Sykes said. 'So, if you're happy, Jenna, we'll make the referral. Though right now,' she added, looking over to where some kind of structure seemed to have been erected in the soft play corner, 'I suspect we have a building to inspect. He's quite the budding archi-tect,' she added to Jenna as we all stood up.

Jenna grinned and pointed. 'More Bob the Builder, I reckon.'

But I could see her whole body swell with pride.

'You know, my son Kieron has autism,' I told her, once we were on our way home. 'He was diagnosed when he was small – with what was then called Asperger's syndrome, which is a mild form of autism. They don't call it that anymore – now they just refer to people being on the autism spectrum.'

'ASD,' she said. 'That's what my friend says her son has. That he has an autism spectrum disorder. She doesn't like the word "disorder" though. I mean, you wouldn't, would you? It's just being a bit different, isn't it? Not a disorder.' What a long way the world has come, I thought. This was so heartening to hear. 'So is he okay, your son?' she asked.

'Kieron? He's fine. If you met him, you probably wouldn't even realise,' I told her. 'He has his funny little ways, but it hasn't stopped him doing anything.' It hit me then how in all these weeks (Where were we – eight weeks? Or was it more now? It was all becoming such a blur) that she had yet to even meet him. Or Lauren, or Riley and David, and all the grandchildren. And though I hardly dared pre-empt fate by anticipating the outcome, if she didn't lose the kids, and they decided to extend the placement, she could do a lot worse than spend some time with the wider family. Well, as long as we could keep Seth's swearing under control.

'You'll have to meet him,' I told her. 'You'll like him. He's funny. And he and Seth would get on like a house on fire.'

And then I regretted having said anything, as I could see her face fall, just a little. It would be as much on her mind now, I reminded myself, as it ever was, perhaps more so. Because, referral or otherwise, she could still have it all taken away from her.

Chapter 23

The court hearing date had been set for the following Thursday. And was first on the schedule, which meant another early start.

'You know,' I said to Mike, as I drew back the curtains to reveal another inky, depressing sky, 'I think I need one of those daylight bulb alarm clocks – the ones that light up slowly, over half an hour, so you can ease into the day. It's such a rude awakening, getting up in the dark.'

'Lightweight,' he said, laughing. 'Welcome to my world, love. Though you're right. It has been a wake-up call, hasn't it? Being back in a world that's dictated by a baby's internal clock. Though, I have to say, I haven't found it nearly as arduous as I expected. Not in that way, at least, which shows we're not quite decrepit yet.'

I pulled on my dressing gown, contemplating the big day ahead. No, we weren't, but I was at least settled on one thing I must do. Remind Christine to remind me that she'd been right in the first place. And to do so, very firmly, as often as she needed to, if I so much as squeaked a suggestion that I might be up for doing one again. Because the emotional strain was just too intense. In a few hours Jenna's future – with or without her children – would be decided, and the anxiety was sitting like a stone in my stomach, because I had no idea how it was going to go.

We'd been given conflicting information, as well. As I'd been told, Lizzie Croft had taken over Sam Burdett's caseload, and had evidently immersed herself in all the finer details – my reports, of course, and all the other evidence – because a couple of days later, she was on the phone to me. And not just to arrange to come and visit Seth and Tommy, for her first routine visit as their new social worker. She'd also called to give me a short inter-rogation (though her word was 'chat') about why and how there had been this new development with Jenna – that her solicitor was now asking for another option to be considered.

'Because it's likely to hold everything up,' she reminded me. 'Were you aware this was happening?' I told her I was. There was a pause. 'And do you know how that came about?'

I knew I had to answer that without fudging the truth, because, at least according to the powers that be at the council, I was already sailing too close to the wind. And I couldn't lie – it was me who had suggested it.

'I asked Sam Burdett if there were any other options available to her,' I said. 'And, after some deliberating, he admitted there were. And when Jenna asked me about them, of course I had to tell her. That was the extent of my involvement. From there it was her solicitor who decided there might be a case for considering one of them, as an alternative if she doesn't win the kids back outright.'

'Which you know is unlikely,' Lizzie said.

'Yes, of course. And I've already told Jenna that if the courts do agree an extension then we're happy to keep her with us a while longer. Though I'm not tempting fate by imagining it's likely. We'll just have to see what today brings.'

'Well, judging by the reports you've sent in this last week, it sounds like she's been doing all the right things, at least. Though, as I've already said, whatever today brings, it's unlikely that we're going to get a decision straight away.'

But Jenna's solicitor, who called later, apparently begged to differ, telling Jenna he knew the presiding judge pretty well, and that if the council didn't win their immediate adoption order then she'd almost certainly, assuming she agreed to considering options, make her decision and act on it straight away.

Naturally, I preferred to believe the solicitor was the right one, as it would at least put an end to the uncertainty.

And now the day was here – a day that for me would mean childcare, as Jenna was being picked up before Seth was due in school, and I'd be in charge of the children for the whole day.

Mommy, Please Don't Leave

While Mike tiptoed downstairs – no point in waking Seth yet – I quickly showered and dressed, tied my hair into a loose ponytail, and threw on my usual baby-minding uniform of long top and leggings. Then I headed downstairs, only to bump into Jenna coming out of the kitchen, wet hair dripping onto a towel over her shoulders.

'Oh, you're up,' I said. 'I thought you'd grab at least another half an hour yet.'

'I needed to iron my new top and wash my hair,' she said, 'so I have time to dry it before Seth's up. I hope you don't mind, but I did it over the kitchen sink, so I didn't wake you guys banging around up in the bathroom.'

'Oh, you're a little love,' I said. 'But we wouldn't have minded.'

'It's fine. Tommy's up. Are you okay to mind him now for me so I can get myself ready?'

'Of course, love,' I said. 'You go ahead.'

Though it seemed Mike was one step ahead of me. He'd made me a coffee but was now busy entertaining the baby, raising him up and down above his head, trying to make him laugh. 'Just thought I'd have a quick cuddle before I set off to work. After all,' he said, lowering his voice a little, 'he might not be here when I get home.'

'Oh, love, don't say that!' I said. 'Don't give up hope. I refuse to believe the judge will agree to adoption. I just can't. It would be just too cruel.'

'But it *might* happen. There's no getting away from that, love. I don't want to sound like the prophet of doom here, but you can't get away from reality. God, I'll miss this little one, though. My little mate –' he said, gurning at Tommy. Who, as had been the case for a couple of weeks now, rewarded Mike with his best and brightest smile. And no wonder, I reflected, as they continued their up-and-down game, because they'd really formed a bond. And was it any wonder? Time and again during this placement, Mike had been the one holding the baby. Seth causing a huge scene? Pass Tommy to Mike. Jenna kicking off? Pass Tommy to Mike. Professionals arriving for a meeting? Pass Tommy to Mike. I had been so blindsided by all the drama, I hadn't seen how protective and close my own husband had become with that little baby. Suddenly, I felt very foolish.

I watched him kiss Tommy gently and pop him back in his baby seat. And could have cried. I was used to getting all hurt and upset when children left us, but this attachment was one that I hadn't even noticed. I mentally crossed my fingers even more.

But I didn't have time to dwell, and I was kind of glad about it, because as soon as Mike left, I heard Seth yelling from upstairs.

'Mummy! Mummy! I need a carry! My legs have been shot off.' Now, that I wouldn't miss. Except I would.

From then on it was a flurry of activity, getting Seth fed and dressed for nursery, while Jenna straightened her hair and did her make-up, and entertaining Baby Tommy as I did so. I had him just about ready to pop into his pram, when the doorbell went. Not a cab, but one of Jenna's solicitor's colleagues, from whom she'd managed to blag a lift, to save the taxi fare. 'Gotta save the pennies,' she'd quipped.

'Right then,' she said, patting herself down. 'Have I got everything?'

'You have, love.'

'Do I look okay?'

'You look beautiful.'

'No, do I look *okay*? As in like a responsible adult.'

'That too. Come on, here's your bag. Now *go*!'

'One more kiss from my babies.' She hugged and kissed Seth and Tommy – the latter in my arms. Then Seth, perhaps tuning into the seriousness of the situation, had a wobble, flinging his arms around her legs. 'Mummy, please don't leave us!'

'I'm not leaving you, you noodle! I'm just going to a very important meeting. I'll be back before you know it,' she added. 'And don't play Casey up, you hear? Or there will definitely be consequences. Right then,' she finished, looking a good couple of inches taller, somehow. 'I'm ready. I promise I'll ring you whenever I can,' she said to me. 'And let you know how things are going.'

And then she was gone, leaving me home alone with the children. Thankfully, her words to Seth seemed to have done the trick, and he behaved beautifully all the way to school. Maybe it was because his mum had come home the last time, just as she had told him she would, but I also had an inkling that he trusted her, period.

That, tiny bit by tiny bit, she was taking control. Which in itself made him feel more secure.

I had no such childish innocence to fall back on. The truth was that it could still go against her and if it did – hard though it was to even think it – there was a chance that Jenna might *not* come home to her kids today. Not in the way Seth assumed, anyway. Yes, she'd come back, because all her belongings were here, but if the decision was made to put the children up for adoption, there was a chance that they would decide to remove them immediately. And it was chilling to reflect that even as I had the thought, someone (or someones) might, probably would, already be on standby to take them. Not before she could say goodbye – no one would be that cruel – but the protocol would be heartbreaking even so. I'd get a call to tell me in advance that Jenna was being escorted home to say goodbye to them, and, as if that wasn't brutal enough, she would then be taken from the house with her belongings and offered a lift to her flat, leaving her babies behind with me until social workers arrived to take them.

It would then get even worse. Given the complication of Seth's challenging behaviours, an assessment would take place to see if they should be adopted together, or whether they'd be better off going to different parents. I could hardly bear to think that they might get split up, but the reality was that almost everyone wanted babies, rather less their challenging four-year-old brothers.

And just the thought of the aftermath – me in my

empty house, Jenna in her empty flat and two bewildered children, perhaps in different homes, once again with strangers – was too much to think about. So I made myself stop. This was *way* too much reality to cope with.

And it wouldn't do. I needed to keep myself focussed, and not transmit so much of a smidge of my anxiety to Seth. I scooped him up in my arms, before sending him in to Mrs Sykes.

'Didn't Mummy look beautiful for her meeting?' I asked him. 'And you know something, Seth? You look just like her.'

He treated me to a huge smile. 'She *did*,' he declared. 'And me and my brother are the spit and dab of her.'

I laughed at the old-fashioned expression. It was one I hadn't heard in many, many years. 'So you are,' I agreed. 'Three peas in a pod.'

I could only hope it would still be the same pod by the time the day was over.

Chapter 24

By the time my mobile rang – as late as 5.15 p.m. – Mike was home, Tyler was home, and I was almost at breaking point.

It was an unknown number, too. Not Jenna. Which terrified me. Particularly since I hadn't heard from her since just after lunch, at which point she had no idea how things were going to go for her.

I called for hush – Tyler and Seth were running riot with a pair of plastic swords Tyler had bought him the previous day – my head already filled with a single, sharp vision. Of Jenna being led away, handcuffed, from a dock.

Which was utterly ridiculous. She wasn't the defendant in a murder trial, for God's sake! But Mike brought me back to reality.

'Answer that bloody phone, woman!'

So I did, my heart drumming in my chest. Because this had to be bad news, surely? I took myself off into the living room, and shut the door.

'Mrs Watson? This is Jules Hammond. I'm a clerk at Ernest Fleming & Co. Solicitors.'

Jenna's solicitors. 'Yes, that's me,' I said. 'Is everything okay?'

'Yes, yes, everything is fine,' she assured me breezily. 'Jenna's being debriefed in a meeting room with her solicitor at the moment, but she asked that I phone you to let you know the outcome of today.'

'So the judge has made her decision?'

'Yes, she has.' So they were right. The authority wrong. No delay. 'And you'll be pleased to hear we got what we'd asked for.'

'She won her case?' I asked, as Mike slipped into the room behind me.

'Not quite,' the clerk said. 'It was more that the local authority *didn't* win. The children will remain in care but living with mother.'

I did a double take. Had I misheard? 'Hang on – wait,' I said. 'In care, living with mother?'

'Yes. In care, living with mother. There are obviously a lot of logistics to work out, but the social workers are putting together a plan as we speak. And I'm quite sure they never had one, because they were definitely not expecting this outcome, but anyway, it is what it is. They'll catch up soon enough. Are you alright keeping the family until after the weekend, so Jenna has time to get organised? We'll need to confirm that's the case to the judge.'

'Oh goodness, yes, of course,' I said. 'They can stay as long as they need to.'

'Excellent,' the clerk said. 'I'll let everyone know that. We shouldn't be too much longer now. I'm sure Jenna will call to let you know when she's on her way back.'

I rang off in a state of utter confusion, only compounded when a text notification popped up on my screen. From Emma. *Yayyy!!! Brilliant news! You must be sooo relieved!!!!*

'In care, living with mother?' Mike kept his voice down. As, of course, he would, because it wasn't for us to tell Seth the news. That job was for Jenna. As now, on the face of it, would be every job, every decision, to do with her children. As of now, give or take the odd bit of paperwork, we were no longer fostering Seth and Tommy.

I nodded. 'That's what they said. She's going home. After the weekend, apparently – well, I guess as soon as she's organised. What's that about? I thought they were making an application to extend the placement *here*.'

Mike shrugged. 'I've no idea, love. Perhaps they felt this was the better option.'

'But why didn't Jenna say anything? As far as I knew she wanted to stay *here*.'

'Perhaps she changed her mind.'

'She must have. Or maybe she didn't. Perhaps the authority argued against her staying here. Oh, God. Do you think that might be it? That they think she's more likely to fail if she's on her own? Do you think that's it? Because that's pretty much what Sam Burdett intimated.

286

That there was no benefit in her staying here and dragging everything out if the end result was going to be that they got their adoption order anyway.'

Mike placed an arm around my shoulder. 'You are a case, Case,' he told me. 'Stop flipping hypothesising! We'll know when she gets here, won't we? And it could be that this was exactly what Jenna was going for all along. Have you thought of that?'

'Er, hello?' I harrumphed. 'I thought you said to stop hypothesising?'

I was stunned. There were no two ways about it. The one option I had dismissed as so unlikely as not to be even up for consideration (well, apart from Jenna legally getting the children back, which was never going to happen) had turned out to be the one Jenna's solicitor had not only pressed for but got. Had this been Jenna's idea? Was that really what she wanted? To go home, with her two little ones, to live on her own – and with a level of input from social services that would make even the most confident mother feel intimidated and scrutinised? I couldn't quite believe she'd have chosen that option. To me, bar, of course, losing the kids altogether, it felt like the worst of all worlds. An intensely high-risk strategy, with no safety net. So had it been settled on with the authority's input, based on their assumption that if she stayed with me I might allow her too much latitude? That things would just drag on towards the same inevitable end?

No, no and no. It was not that, it *was* Jenna. I could tell the very moment she came through the door, some forty-five minutes later. A brief moment of uncomfortable eye contact – on her part, at least – that immediately gave me the answer, before she dumped her bag and squatted down in the hall to let Seth run into her arms.

'Oh, I've missed you, you little munchkin,' she said, burying her face in his hair. Tufty now, growing out, measuring the passage of time. 'Did Aunty Casey tell you the good news?'

'What news?' he said. Behind him, I shook my head.

'We're going home,' she said. 'Back to *our* home.'

'And my brother?'

She grinned at him. 'Of *course* your brother! We can't leave him behind, can we?'

'Alright. That's okay,' Seth replied philosophically. 'But what about the telly? Can we get a special telly like the one in the big room?'

'Maybe not *right* away, I'm afraid,' she told him. 'But as soon as we can, I promise.' She stood up again, smiled at the four of us, gathered in the hallway. Mike, holding Tommy, Tyler and me. 'Well,' she said, 'that was *quite* a day!' Then, almost as if she needed to set a maternal precedent, held her hands out, as any mother would, to take charge of her younger son.

'I'll bet,' I said. 'Coffee?'

She smiled and shook her head. Then bent down to retrieve something from her capacious handbag. 'I thought we should celebrate, so I bought some Prosecco.

Just a glass for me, mind.' She grinned. 'Can't afford a sore head!'

There was little time to talk then, as there were children to get organised. Seth still had another day in nursery the following morning. His last one. No doubt social services would be getting into gear now on that front; they obviously had a duty to get him into another nursery immediately, and I was glad that Mrs Sykes had moved to act when she did, because it didn't matter that Seth would be starting at a new place – he would still be in the system, which was the most important thing, whether the actual referral took a few weeks or a few months. In the meantime, however, for one more day only, our morning routine would remain in place. And, happily, the bedtime routine was without drama, both Seth and Tommy settling without a fuss, and – I might have imagined it, but I was pretty sure I didn't – Jenna lingering rather longer in the conservatory with Tommy than she usually did, before re-emerging and joining Mike and I in the living room, to tell us all about her day in court.

Which she did, with no small degree of feeling.

'Oh, you should have heard the solicitor for the social,' she said. 'She was making me out to be *such* a criminal. Bringing up all my past, my drug taking, and stealing and stuff. Then she said about prison, and I was, like, gobsmacked, listening to her. She made out like I'd decided I didn't want to look after Tommy – like I had fobbed him off on you, when it was the exact opposite of that! I did it because I thought it would be better for *him*! She was so *horrid*. Honestly, listening to her, I really thought it was all over.'

Mike and I exchanged covert smiles as we listened to her ranting. The judge had clearly seen something in Jenna that she liked, that she believed in – and perhaps it was this; this passion to win her kids back at all costs, to prove to the world that she *could* be a mum. Whatever it had been, I was just so relieved and happy that fate had decreed it be this judge, on this day. Yes, she had a long way to go and lots to learn, but this girl *did* love her children, and there was no doubt about that, not in my mind, at least. And with the right help and guidance she could surely learn how to be a decent parent, if not a perfect one. Because none of us were that. We were all guilty of making mistakes. It's just that most of us can reflect on our pasts, our own childhoods, and hopefully take lessons from that. Jenna didn't have that – she had no role models at all.

'I can imagine,' I said to her. 'But they're just doing what they're paid to do – fighting the other "team". And the judge would have been used to it. This is how the courts work. And don't forget, she has all the evidence, so she can take a balanced view.'

'And it sounds like your man did a pretty good job too,' Mike added. 'Because in spite of what that solicitor said, the judge decided to give you a chance anyway, so she must believe in you, love, like we all do.'

Jenna beamed. 'She was brilliant. I mean, I know I don't listen to everything said to me, especially if it's all big words and shit, but she said some really nice things about me. It was almost like she was talking about someone else. She said I'm a good mum. And she said your daily sheets were evidence of that, Casey, so thank you for that. It really means a lot to me. And I know I've got lots of shit to do and prove over the next year, but I swear down, I will not waste this chance. That's what it is, that's what the judge said; that it's a chance to prove to everyone that I really want to change and make a good life for my family.'

'And you will, darling,' I said, unable to resist going across to the armchair and giving her a big hug. 'We know you can do it, Jen, and I'll still be here, at the end of the phone if you want to chat or rant or whatever. When you leave us, that won't be the end of it, you know.'

'Really?' She looked surprised. 'You mean I can still see you and everything?'

'Are you kidding?' Mike said. 'Of course you can still see us! They don't put us in a crate at the end of every placement and ship us off to the Maldives. Haha – chance would be a fine thing!'

It was at that moment, Jenna close to tears, that Tyler popped his head round the door. 'I'm off to Naomi's now,' he said. 'And I might be late back. See you all tomorrow, yeah?'

At which Jenna immediately leapt from her chair. 'Hang on,' she said. 'I've got something for you and

Naomi. You know, to say sorry for all that stupid kicking-off a couple of weeks ago.'

She disappeared back into the conservatory, then came back out with a little bag. A little gold and black bag bearing a familiar logo. She held it out to Tyler. 'There's one for each of you. I got the solicitor to run me round to the shops while we were waiting at lunchtime. I don't know if it's your thing or not, but, well –'

Tyler took the bag. 'So can I open mine now?'

'Course,' she said. 'Yours is the one in the black tissue. Naomi's is the other one. More girly.'

Tyler opened the tissue to reveal a slim brown leather bracelet, with a tiny silver heart hanging from it.

'Hope it's not too cringe-worthy,' Jenna said. 'There's a heart on hers too.'

'No, it's sick,' he said. 'Perfect. *Thank* you. But you didn't need to do that. You need to save your money, don't you? Anyway, thank you,' he said again. 'That's really thoughtful.'

Typical Jenna, I thought. Generous to a fault, no regard for saving. 'It didn't cost much,' she said, as if reading my thoughts. 'They were in a mid-season sale. Anyway, I hope Naomi likes hers. Something to remember me by. Well, as if being clunked on the head by a Postman Pat van isn't enough, lol!'

'Seriously, love,' I said to her, once Tyler had left. 'That was the sweetest, sweetest thing to do. But you need to be really, really careful with your money now.

Not just because you should, but because it's going to be one of the things they will be monitoring pretty closely now you're going it alone.'

'I *am* careful with money,' she said. 'You don't need to worry on that front. I might be rubbish at lots of things, but I'm not about money. I've had a lifetime to learn how to manage on my own, believe me.' She smiled ruefully. 'Well, apart from that one bit, when I totally lost my shit, and burned through a bloody ton on drugs, obvs.'

'Obvs,' I agreed, smiling. 'And that's really good to know.'

She looked down, and then up again. At both me and Mike. 'And I'm sorry,' she said.

'Sorry?'

'For not telling you. That I planned on leaving. I wanted to, but I was worried that you'd try to talk me out of it. And you might have, because it does feel bloody scary. I mean, there was also the fact that I didn't even dare *hope* that they wouldn't take them away from me altogether. But as soon as you told me it was one of the options I knew it was the one I had to try for. You do understand, don't you?'

'Absolutely,' Mike said, before I could.

'I mean, I've loved it here, *really*,' she said, 'and even if I might not have sounded it sometimes, I'm *so* grateful to you both for taking us all in. For looking after Seth and Tommy when I couldn't. For putting up with all my shit. And I know it must seem like I'm not – that I can't wait to be out of here – but, actually I can't. But that's not because of you.'

'We understand, love,' I began. 'You need your own space, we get that.'

'But it's not so much that,' she said, 'my flat's, like, super-tiny. It's just that if I don't, it's like I can't start being a proper mum again. Specially to Seth. It's like *you're* his mum and dad and I'm, like, his sister, or his aunty. And the longer that goes on, the harder it's going to be for him to get used to the life he's *really* going to be living.' She glanced around her then. '*My* life. No big magic telly. At least not yet. And Emma said to me today – did I tell you she came? – that the biggest thing now is that the buck stops with me.' She smiled. 'I don't know what the buck is exactly, but you know what I mean?'

'I know exactly what you mean,' I said. And I did.

'So, I was thinking, I mean, I don't want to mess up your weekend or anything, but d'you think we might be able to get us moved back in on Saturday? I mean, that flat's not going to be in the best state after being empty all this time, and, er, it's not like I'm the world's greatest cleaner or anything, so it's not exactly tidy … but I was thinking, Casey, maybe if you could drop me and Tommy off there after we drop Seth to nursery tomorrow morning, I could at least make a start, and –'

Mike burst out laughing. 'Drop you off? You've as much chance of Casey dropping you off to clean your flat as flying, love, I promise you.'

'If it's too much trouble –'

Mommy, Please Don't Leave

'*Trouble?* Trust me, you'll have to beat her off with a stick.'

I did jazz hands. 'Guilty as charged. World's Greatest Cleaner.'

'So, do you think she'll be okay?' Mike said, as we lay in bed that night. 'Tell me honestly. Do you have faith in her? Do you think she can do it? It's one thing to cope while she's here, with us supporting her, quite another to be a single mum in a flat with two little ones, and social services constantly breathing down your neck.'

'Honestly? I don't know,' I said. 'I'm sure she doesn't even know herself yet. How can anyone? It's going to be tough for her. But at least she *does* have social services breathing down her neck. I mean, you can look at it in two ways – as a help or a hindrance. I think in her case, it will actually be a help. A support network. And, let's face it, if she can keep her children, that's got to be better for them, hasn't it? And it's Lizzie Croft who's going to be their social worker now, isn't it? Plus, she has Emma to support her, if she needs it. And us, don't forget.'

'Ah,' he said, 'speaking of which, I lied to Jenna earlier.'

'Lied? About what?'

'About them not packing us into a crate and shipping us off to the Maldives.' He reached across to his bedside table and flipped open the cover on his tablet. 'For a week, at least,' he said. 'I was thinking Easter. Maybe April.'

I snuggled up, sighing happily, as the screen came to life. He started scrolling. He'd already been doing his research, clearly. Blue skies, bright sun, turquoise seas … the Spanish flag?

'Pick a Costa,' he said. 'We can't run to the Maldives.'

Epilogue

Jenna and the boys left us, in the end, on the Sunday. It taking a good deal longer than she'd imagined to lick her flat into shape – well, to my own exacting standards, at any rate. And Seth left Tyler a present. One of his two plastic swords, so 'we can both play polices at the same time each day, and you can be the good guy if you want to'.

That was actually very generous of Seth – and also thoughtful. He *never* allowed anyone to be a good guy. Other people were always designated either as bad guys or polices. Despite Tyler constantly trying to play a 'good pirate', or a 'brave soldier', it had simply never happened. He was bad and had to be punished and that was that.

I took Seth's newfound empathy as a win, just as I'd had to do with any tiny steps forward he'd made, and knowing that professionals were now going to be heavily involved in his life, I felt positive for the family's future. I was also heartened to hear, after only a couple of weeks, that an appointment was in the process of being set up for Seth, for an initial sit-down with a child psychologist.

Over the next few weeks there were, of course, teething problems. Jenna would phone me up at least twice-weekly, voicing her rage at social services, saying they were poking their noses into her business all the time and trying to tell her how best to look after her babies. So I'd calm her down, gently reminding her this was their job, and that she'd signed up to it to avoid the possibility of losing her family altogether. Still, it was upsetting for her, because it meant she never really felt in control, and with people always pointing out that this wasn't the end of the road – there was still a long way to go before she was trusted enough to be left alone – she often felt inadequate and scared.

But perhaps that wasn't such a bad thing. Because over time she began to realise that there *was* a way to go still, which led her to accept more help from the various outside agencies. I knew she had been going to domestic violence sessions and parenting classes, but it surprised me when she told me she'd also been attending weekly sessions with a counsellor. She'd set it up by herself, without any prompting from social workers – to try to heal herself, she told me. That really impressed me. I later heard on the grapevine that her new family support worker was super-impressed too, so much so that she felt inspired enough to take Jenna along to a different parenting class, and have her help facilitate a Q & A session for other teenage parents – something I knew would really empower her.

True to her word, Jenna and I would meet up once a month to go for a coffee or take the kids to the park. It was during one of these outings that she surprised me even more.

'I'm writing a book,' she said. 'Seriously. It's a bit rubbish – I can't write nearly well enough because I was hardly in school. But the counsellor suggested I should start writing about my childhood, as a way to help process it and let it go. And now I've started I can't seem to stop!' She then handed me a sheaf of paper – copies of what looked like an exercise book, complete with scribbled doodles in the corners. 'Not now, though. Too embarrassing. Read it later, yeah? I just wanted you to know all the things I was running away from. The stuff I didn't tell you. And you never know, it might help someone else like me, one day.'

So I read it, and my heart broke for this girl all over again, because for all that I did know, what I didn't know was even more tragic. Not expected. Never wanted. Never loved. Never cherished. Born to the wrong parents, at the wrong time, in the wrong place. A story that we've all heard a thousand times before. But still unique to this girl. Her personal cross to bear and her story to tell. I'm so glad she's rewriting her future.

* * *

So where are they now? Well, two years down the line, Baby Tommy is about to start nursery, and Jenna has just got herself a part-time job. She'd been volunteering for over a year at a local clinic, and found she really enjoyed it, and is now a healthcare assistant for a local NHS hospital. She has a new man in her life – who also works hard, as an apprentice plumber – and little Seth, now six, and with a statement of special educational needs, has a dedicated teaching assistant to support him in his local school. He is doing so well, and though he still has his bad days, and probably always will, he is nowhere near as challenging as he used to be.

When he grows up, he wants to be a policeman.

CASEY WATSON

One woman determined to
make a difference.

Read Casey's poignant
memoirs and be inspired.

LET ME GO

Harley is an anxious teen
who wants to end her own life,
and there's only one woman
who can find out why

Casey makes a breakthrough which
sheds light on the disturbing truth –
there is a man in Harley's life, a
very dangerous man indeed.

A DARK SECRET

A troubled nine-year-old with
a violent streak, Sam's relentless
bullying sees even his siblings beg
not to be placed with him

When Casey delves into Sam's past
she uncovers something far darker
than she had imagined.

A BOY WITHOUT HOPE

A history of abuse and neglect
has left Miller destined for
life's scrap heap

Miller's destructive behaviour will push
Casey to her limits, but she is determined
to help him overcome his demons
and give him hope.

NOWHERE TO GO

Eleven-year-old Tyler has stabbed his stepmother and has nowhere to go

With his birth mother dead and a father who doesn't want him, what can be done to stop his young life spiralling out of control?

GROOMED

Keeley is urgently rehomed with Casey after accusing her foster father of abuse

It's Casey's job to keep Keeley safe, but can she protect this strong-willed teen from the dangers online?

THE SILENT WITNESS

Bella's father is on a ventilator, fighting for his life, while her mother is currently on remand in prison, charged with his attempted murder

Bella is the only witness.

RUNAWAY GIRL

Adrianna arrives on Casey's doorstep with no possessions, no English and no explanation

It will be a few weeks before Casey starts getting the shocking answers to her questions . . .

MUMMY'S LITTLE SOLDIER

Leo isn't a bad lad, but his frequent absences from school mean he's on the brink of permanent exclusion

Leo is clearly hiding something, and Casey knows that if he is to have any kind of future, it's up to her to find out the truth.

SKIN DEEP

Flip is being raised by her alcoholic mother, and comes to Casey after a fire at their home

Flip has Foetal Alcohol Syndrome (FAS), but it soon turns out that this is just the tip of the iceberg . . .

A STOLEN CHILDHOOD

Kiara appears tired and distressed, and the school wants Casey to take her under her wing for a while

On the surface, everything points to a child who is upset that her parents have separated. The horrific truth, however, shocks Casey to the core.

THE GIRL WITHOUT A VOICE

What is the secret behind Imogen's silence?

Discover the shocking and devastating past of a child with severe behavioural problems.

A LAST KISS FOR MUMMY

A teenage mother and baby in need of a loving home

At fourteen, Emma is just a child herself – and one who's never been properly mothered.

BREAKING THE SILENCE

Two boys with an unlikely bond

With Georgie and Jenson, Casey is facing her toughest test yet.

MUMMY'S LITTLE HELPER

A young girl secretly caring for her mother

Abigail has been dealing with pressures no child should face. Casey has the difficult challenge of helping her to learn to let go.

TOO HURT TO STAY

Branded 'vicious and evil', eight-year-old Spencer asks to be taken into care

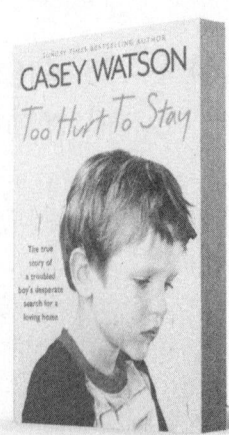

Casey and her family are disgusted: kids aren't born evil. Despite the challenges Spencer brings, they are determined to help him find a loving home.

LITTLE PRISONERS

Abused siblings who do not know what it means to be loved

With new-found security and trust, Casey helps Ashton and Olivia to rebuild their lives

CRYING FOR HELP

A damaged girl haunted by her past

Sophia pushes Casey to the limits, threatening the safety of the whole family. Can Casey make a difference in time?

THE BOY NO ONE LOVED

Five-year-old Justin was desperate and helpless

Six years after being taken into care, Justin has had 20 failed placements. Casey and her family are his last hope.

TITLES AVAILABLE AS E-BOOK ONLY

AT RISK

Adam is brought to Casey while his mum
recovers in hospital – just for a few days

But a chance discovery reveals that Casey has stumbled upon
something altogether more sinister . . .